Introduction

Food Finder

Grand Melbourne dining	16
Business dining	26
Melbourne's Bayside pub scene	36
Dining on the move	46
The Queen Victoria Market	56
Little Vietnam	66
Victorian wines	76
Gourmet country retreats	86

Our choice:

Central City (CBD) — 8

Restaurants	8
Bars, cafés and pubs	13
Shops, markets and picnic sites	15

Southbank — 18

Restaurants	18
Bars, cafés and pubs	23
Shops, markets and picnic sites	25

St Kilda and Bayside — 28

Restaurants	29
Bars, cafés and pubs	33
Shops, markets and picnic sites	35

Bars, cafés and pubs	42
Shops, markets and picnic sites	44

Carlton and Lygon St — 48

Restaurants	49
Bars, cafés and pubs	52
Shops, markets and picnic sites	54

Fitzroy: Brunswick St and Smith St — 58

Restaurants	59
Bars, cafés and pubs	62
Shops, markets and picnic sites	64

The Yarra Valley — 68

Restaurants	69
Bars, cafés and pubs	72
Shops, markets and picnic sites	74

Around Port Phillip Bay — 78

Restaurants	78
Bars, cafés and pubs	82
Shops, markets and picnic sites	84

Food etiquette and culture	88
Menu decoder	90
Recipes	94
Acknowledgements	96

INTRODUCTION

Time for Food guides are designed to help you find interesting and enjoyable places to eat in the world's main tourist destinations. Each guide divides the destination into eight areas. Each area has a map, followed by a selection of the restaurants, cafés, bars, pubs and food markets in that area. The aim is to cover the whole spectrum of food establishments, from gourmet temples to humble cafés, plus good food shops or delicatessens where you can buy picnic ingredients or food to cook yourself.

If you are looking for a particular restaurant, regardless of its location, or a particular type of cuisine, you can turn to the Food Finder, starting on page 4. This lists all the establishments reviewed in this guide by name (in alphabetical order) and then by cuisine type.

PRICES

Unlike some guides, we have not wasted space telling you how bad a restaurant is – bad or poor-value restaurants simply do not make it into the guide. Many other guides ask restaurants to pay for their entries, or expect the restaurant to advertise in return for a listing. We do neither of these things: the restaurants and cafés

▲ Southgate dining scene

featured here simply represent a selection of places that the author has sampled and enjoyed.

If there is one consistent criterion for inclusion in the guide, it is good value. Good value does not, of course, necessarily mean cheap. Food lovers know the difference between a restaurant where the high prices are fully justified by the quality of the ingredients and the excellence of the cooking and presentation of the food, and meretricious establishments where high prices are merely the result of pretentious attitudes.

Some of the restaurants featured here are undeniably expensive if you consume caviar and champagne, but even haute cuisine establishments offer set-price menus (especially at lunchtime) allowing budget diners to enjoy dishes created by top chefs and every bit as good as those on the regular menu. At the same time, some of the eating places listed here might not make it into more conventional food guides, because they are relatively humble cafés or takeaways. Some are deliberately oriented towards tourists, but there is nothing wrong in that: what some guides dismiss as 'tourist traps' may be deservedly popular for providing choice and good value.

FEEDBACK

You may or may not agree with the author's choice – in either case we would like to know about your experiences. Any feedback you give us and any recommendations you make will be followed up, so that you can look forward to seeing your restaurant suggestions in print in the next edition.

Feedback forms have been included at the back of the book and you can e-mail us with comments by writing to: *timeforfood@thomascook.com*. Let us know what you like or do not like about the restaurants featured here.

Tell us if you discover shops, pubs, cafés, bars, restaurants or markets that you think should go in the guide. No food guide can keep pace with the changing restaurant scene, as chefs move on, establishments open or close, and menus, opening hours or credit card details change. Let us know if you discover changes – say to telephone numbers or opening times.

Symbols used in this guide

VISA	Visa accepted
Diners Club	Diners Club accepted
MasterCard	MasterCard accepted
🍴	Restaurant
🍷	Bar, café or pub
🧺	Shop, market or picnic site
✆	Telephone
🚉	Transport
❷	Numbered red circles relate to the maps at the start of the section

The price indications used in this guide have the following meanings:

$	budget level
$$	typical/average for the destination
$$$	up-market

Introduction | 3

FOOD FINDER

RESTAURANTS A–Z

A
Abla's 49
Akvavit 18
Arthurs 78

B
Il Bacaro Cucina e Bar 8
The Baths 78
The Beach House 79
Becco 8
Bedi's 29
Bistro '1' 9
Bistro Vite 18
Blakes 19
De Bortoli Winery Restaurant 69
Breezes 19

C
Café Coco 59
Café di Stasio 29
Le Café Francais 49
Café Grossi 39
Castle Restaurant at Peppers Delgany 79
Caterina's Cucina e Bar 27
Cecconi's 20
Chinois 39
Chris's Beacon Point Restaurant 87
Circa, the Prince 29
The Colonial Tramcar Restaurant 46

D
Dong Ba '2' 66
Donnini's 49
Donovans 29
The Duck 20

E
Eleonore's at Château Yering 69
est est est 30
Eucalypt Ridge 86
The European 10
The European Grill (EG) 10
Eyton on Yarra 69

F
Fergusson Winery Restaurant 69
The Fitz Café 59
Flower Drum 26
France Soir 39

G
Il Gambero 49
The George Hotel 37
Grossi Florentino 16
Guernica 59
Guru Da Dhaba 59
E Gusto 20

H
Hagger's 40
Harry's 80
Healesville Restaurant and Café 70
The House at Mt Prior 87
Howqua Dale Gourmet Retreat 86

I
Isthmus of Kra 30
Italy '1' 10

J
Jacques Reymond 17
JJ's Champagne Bar and Grill 27
Joe's Garage 50

K
Kazen 60
Koaki Restaurant 80
Koko 21
Kuni's 10

L
Lake House 86
Langton's 26
Lemongrass 50
Lime Restaurant 80
London Hotel 37
Lucky Chan 21
Lynch's 27

M
Madam Fang 11
La Madrague 30
Marchetti's Latin 11
Marchetti Tuscan Grill 11
Marylands Country Hotel 70
Matteo's 60
Maxim's 40
Max's at Red Hill Estate 81
mecca 21
Melbourne Wine Room 30
Mietta's 81
Minh Tan '3' 67
Misuzu's 31
Molly Bloom's 36

N
Near East 31
Da Noi 40

O
The O'Connell Centenary Hotel 36
One Fitzroy St 31
Onions 41

P
Paris-Go Bistro 50
The Point 31
pomme 41
Powerscourt Country House 87
Puffing Billy 47

Q
Quan '88' 66

R
Red Emperor 21
Le Restaurant 11
Riberry Café and Restaurant 70
Ristorante Strega 22
The River Seafood Bar and Grill 22

S
Scusa Mi 22
Sempre Caffe e Paninoteca 81
Shakahari 50
Shark Fin Inn 11
Sicilian Vespers 51
Silks 26
Il Solito Posto 12
Stavros Tavern 32
Stefano's 87
Stella 12
The Stokehouse 32
Strathvea 70
Sud 12

Swallows 37
Sweet Basil 41

T
The Tandoor 41
Tho Tho Bar and Restaurant 67
Thy Thy '1' 66
Tiamo 51
Tolarno Bar and Bistro
Toofey's 51

V
Vegetarian Orgasm 61

W
Warrenmang Vineyard Resort 86
Waterfront 22
Wild Yak 61
Windsor Hotel Grand Ballroom 16

Y
The Yarra Glen Grand Hotel 71
Yering Station Restaurant and Wine Bar 71

BARS, CAFÉS AND PUBS A–Z
189 Espresso Bar 33
292 Wine Bar 52
Arc Café 52
The Argo Inn 42
Arriverderci Aroma 13
Automatic Café 23
Babka's Bakery Café 62
La Baracca Trattoria 82
Bar Corvina 33
Birdcage 33
Black Cat Café 62
Black Spur Nursery and Tea House 72
Blue Train Café 23
The Botanical Hotel 42
Brubakers Bagel Bar 23
Brunetti Caffè 52
Café a taglio 33
Café Barcelona 33
Café e Cucina 42
Café Feedwell 42
Café Pelican 82
Café Racer 33
Café Segovia 13
Café Sweethearts 33
Callis and Forrest 42
Campari's 13
Candy Bar 42

The Carlton Paragon Café 52
Carmen Bar 62
La Casa del Caffè 53
Cervo Café 23
Chinta Blues 34
Church St Gallery and Café 72
Cicciolina 34
The Continental Café 42, 82
Coppins Tearooms 82
La Couronne 42
Couta Caffè 82
The Deck Café 23
Dogs Bar 34
Domain Chandon 72, 77
The Dunes Restaurant 82
Fidel's Cigar Bar 23
Garden Kiosk 42
Gin Palace 13
Giuseppe's 82
Gluttony - It's a Sin 62
The Grace Darling Hotel 62
Greville Bar 43
Gypsy Bar 62
Hairy Canary 13
Harveys 43
The Healesville Hotel 72
Hopetown Tea Rooms 13
Italian Waiters Club 13
Jika Jika Hotel 62
Jimmy Watson's Wine Bar 53
The Kent Hotel 53
Le Kiosk on the Beach 34
Kitten Club 14
Kri Kri 14
Leonardo's Café 82
The Lounge 14
La Luna Bistro 53
Mario's 62
Martha's Tea Room 72
The Max Hotel 82
Meyers Place 14
Mink Bar 34
The Night Cat 62
Nudel Bar 14
Observatory Café 43
De Oliveira's 63
Ozone Hotel 83
Pasta Express 23
Pellegrini's 14
Piccolo 14
Port Pier Café 83
Portsea Pub 83
The Provincial Hotel 63

Punch Lane Wine Bar 14
Queenscliff Terminal Café 83
Retro Café 63
Rhumba's 24
Robert Burns Hotel 63
Ruby Bar 63
Saint Kilda Pier Kiosk 34
Savi Bar and Café 24
Scheherezade Restaurant and Coffee Lounge 34
Shells Café 83
Simply French 24
Singing Gardens Tea Rooms 72
The Smokehouse 83
Soul Food Café 63
Spray Farm Vineyard 83
Sushi Belt 43
Sweetwater Café 72
Toast Café 63
Tokio 14
Trotters 53
Universita Bar and Ristorante 53
Vegie Bar 63
Victory Café 34
Viet's Quan 43
Vue Grand Hotel 83
Walter's Wine Bar 24
Yarra Glen Café and Store 73
Yarra Valley Dairy 73
Yarra Valley Pasta Shop 75
Yelza 63

Food Finder | 5

SHOPS A–Z
Albert Park Deli 35
An Apple A Day 64
Australian Rainbow Trout Farm 74
Babka's Bakery 64
Becco Food Store 15
Bombay Bazaar 64
Bottoms Up Wine 84
Brunetti's 54
Canals 54
Casa del Gelato 54
Charmaine's Ice Cream 25, 64
Daimaru Food Hall 15
David Jones' Food Glorious Food Hall 15
Donati's Fine Meats 54
Donnini's Pasta 54
Edokko Mart 44
Enoteca Sileno 54
Il Fornaio 35
Gateway Bakers 74
Gourmet Yabby Farm 74
Great Eastern Food Centre 15
Greek Deli and Taverna 44
Greens and Grains 44
Grinders Coffee House 54
Haigh's Chocolates 15
Hotsville 44
Jasper's 64
Jonathon's of Collingwood 64
Just Fine Foods 84
Kebab Factory 64
Kennedy and Wilson Chocolate Shop 74
King And Godfree 55
Kinglake Raspberries 74
let's eat 44
Lettuce and Lovage 25
Lilydale Apiaries 74
Lilydale Herb Farm 74
The Lolly Box 25
Maggie's Kitchen 84
Maison de Tunisie 64
Mamma Vittoria Pasta Classica 64
Maroundah Orchards 74
Marrons Glacés 44
Maxim's Cakes 15
Melbourne Cheese House 55
Mondo 84
Montague Park Food Store 35
Myer Food Hall 15
The Nut Shack 25
The Organic Warehouse 64
Organic Wholefoods 65
Paterson's Cakes 44
Pizzetti 25
Q Food Gourmet Deli 84
Queenscliff Seafoods 84
Rathdowne Street Food Store 35
Red Hill Cool Stores 84
Scicluna's of Sorrento 84
Shoji 25
Simon Johnson Fine Foods 65
Sunny Ridge Strawberry Farm 84
Sword's 65
Tea Too (T2) 65
Thresherman's Bakehouse 55
The Upper Crust 65
The Vital Ingredient 35
Walter's Wine and Food Store 25
Yarra Glen Bakehouse 74
Yarra Valley Dairy 74
Yarra Valley Pasta Shop 75
Ye Olde Worlde Lolly Shoppe 85

MARKETS A–Z
Melbourne Organics 35
Prahran Market 44
Queen Victoria Market 56
Red Hill Community Market 85
South Melbourne Market 35
St Andrews Market 75
Yarra Glen Craft Market 75
Yarra Valley Regional Farmers Market 75

PICNIC SITES A–Z
Albert Park Lake 35
Arthurs Seat 85
Badger Weir Reserve 75
Black Spur 75
Carlton Gardens 55
Don Road 75
Healesville Sanctuary 75
Melbourne University 55
Royal Park 55

BEACHES A–Z
Bushrangers Bay 85
Cape Schanck 85
Elwood 35
Geelong Botanic Gardens 85
Mornington Peninsula tip 85
Port Melbourne 35
Red Hill 85
Swan Bay 85

RESTAURANTS BY CUISINE

ASIAN
The Baths 78
Chinois 39
Near East 31

AUSTRALIAN
Arthurs 78
Blakes 19
Breezes 19

6 | Food Finder

Café Coco 59
Castle Restaurant at Peppers Delgany 79
Chris' Beacon Point Restaurant 87
The Colonial Tramcar Restaurant 46
Donovans 29
The Duck 20
Eleonore's at Château Yering 69
Eucalypt Ridge 86
The European Grill (EG) 10
Eyton on Yarra 69
Fergusson Winery Restaurant 69
The Fitz Café 59
The George Hotel 37
Guernica 59
Hagger's 40
Healesville Restaurant and Café 70
The House at Mt Prior 87
Howqua Dale Gourmet Retreat 86
Jacques Reymond 17
Joe's Garage 50
Lake House 86
Lime Restaurant 80
London Hotel 37
Marylands Country Hotel 70
Mietta's 81
One Fitzroy St 31
Onions 41
The Point 31
Powerscourt Country House 87
Puffing Billy 47
Le Restaurant 11
Riberry Café and Restaurant 70
Stella 12
The Stokehouse 32
Strathvea 70
Swallows 37
Tolarno Bar and Bistro
Warrenmang Vineyard Resort 86
The Yarra Glen Grand Hotel 71
Yering Station Restaurant and Wine Bar 71

BRITISH
pomme 41
Windsor Hotel Grand Ballroom 16

CHINESE
Flower Drum 26
Lucky Chan 21
Red Emperor 21
Shark Fin Inn 11
Silks 26

EUROPEAN
Circa, the Prince 29
est est est 30
The European 10

FRENCH
Bistro '1' 9
Bistro Vite 18
Le Café Francais 49
France Soir 39
Jacques Reymond 17
Langton's 26
La Madrague 30
Maxim's 40
Paris-Go Bistro 50

GREEK
Stavros Tavern 32

INDIAN
Bedi's 29
Guru Da Dhaba 59
The Tandoor 41

INTERNATIONAL
JJ's Champagne Bar and Grill 27
Lynch's 27
Madam Fang 11

IRISH
Molly Bloom's 36

ITALIAN
Il Bacaro Cucina e Bar 8
Becco 8
De Bortoli Winery Restaurant 69
Café di Stasio 29
Café Grossi 39
Caterina's Cucina e Bar 27
Cecconi's 20
Donnini's 49
Il Gambero 49
Grossi Florentino 16
E Gusto 20
Italy '1' 10
Marchetti's Latin 11
Marchetti Tuscan Grill 11
Da Noi 40
Ristorante Strega 22
Scusa Mi 22
Sempre Caffe e Paninoteca 81
Sicilian Vespers 51
Il Solito Posto 12
Stefano's 87
Sud 12
Tiamo 51

JAPANESE
Kazen 60
Koaki Restaurant 80
Koko 21
Kuni's 10
Misuzu's 31

LEBANESE
Abla's 49

MEDITERRANEAN
The Baths 78
The Beach House 79
Matteo's 60
Max's at Red Hill Estate 81
mecca 21
Melbourne Wine Room 30
The O'Connell Centenary Hotel 36

SEAFOOD
The Beach House 79
Harry's 80
Lucky Chan 21
The River Seafood Bar and Grill 22
Toofey's 51
Waterfront 22

SWEDISH
Akvavit 18

THAI
Isthmus of Kra 30
Lemongrass 50
Sweet Basil 41

TIBETAN
Wild Yak 61

VEGETARIAN
Shakahari 50
Vegetarian Orgasm 61

VIETNAMESE
Dong Ba '2' 66
Minh Tan '3' 67
Quan '88' 66
Tho Tho Bar and Restaurant 67
Thy Thy '1' 66

Food Finder | 7

Central City (CBD)

The central heart of downtown Melbourne appears at first glance to be just another modern bustling city of skyscrapers. But look upwards to see some of the finest Victorian-period architecture in the world, while its wide tree-lined streets are linked by a honeycomb of lanes and alleys hiding what is reputedly the best collection of restaurants, bars and cafés in Australia.

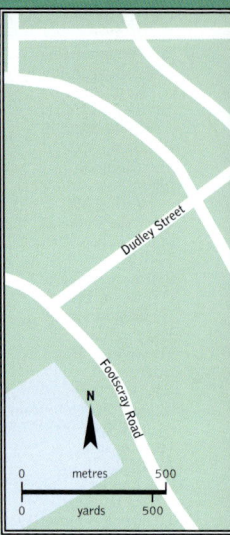

CENTRAL CITY (CBD)
Restaurants

Il Bacaro Cucina e Bar ❶

168–70 Little Collins St, City

✆ 03-9654 6778

🚋 Tram up Collins St to Russell St or tram along Swanston St to the Town Hall

Open: lunch Mon–Fri 1200–1430, dinner Mon–Sat 1800–2300

Reservations recommended

All credit cards accepted

Italian

$$

The name *bacaro* is derived from the famous god of wine, Bacchus, and an old Venetian expression meaning 'to be jolly and to eat and drink in good company'. That really is the essence of Il Bacaro, a slick but small modern Italian restaurant complete with chrome bar, wood panelling, small intimate tables and mood lighting – it has been one of Melbourne's 'in' places since opening five years ago. The food is not cheap, but is cooked delicately, with taste relying on the fresh ingredients rather than too many sauces.

Becco ❷

11–25 Crossley St, City

✆ 03-9663 3000

🚋 Tram up Bourke St to Exhibition St or free city circle tram to Parliament House or train to Parliament House Station

Open: lunch Mon–Fri 1200–1500, dinner daily 1800–2300

8 | Central City (CBD)

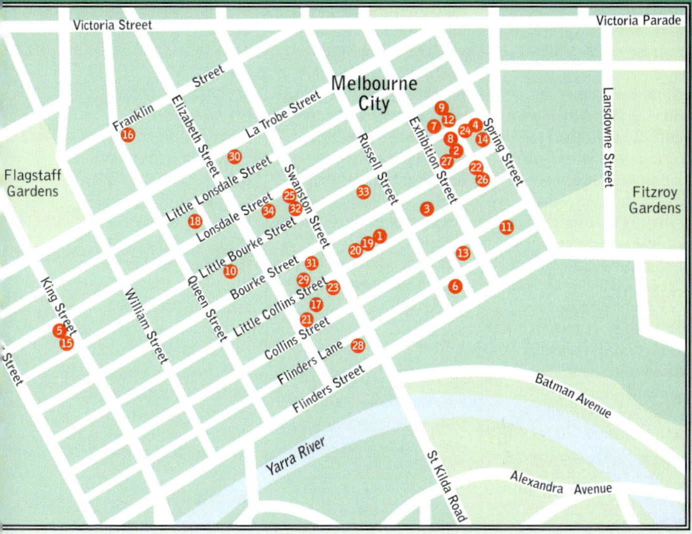

Reservations essential

All credit cards accepted

Italian

$ $

There is a trendy buzz about Becco that four years of success has not been able to dull or tarnish. Serving simple, modern Italian food, Becco is a place to be seen. This is no quiet, sophisticated restaurant; only come here if you love a bit of noise and glamour with your risotto, *gnocchi* or simple Italian-style fish cooking. Don't forget to try the Becco Macchiato at the bar, either – a tall mix of refreshing vodka, Campari, tonic and lime juice.

Bistro 1 ❸

126 Little Collins St, City

✆ 03-9654 3343

🚋 Tram up Collins St to Russell St

Open: Mon–Fri 0830–2230, Sat 1800–2200

▲ Becco

Reservations recommended

All credit cards accepted

French

$ $

Bistro 1 has perfected the art of turning a French bistro into an

Central City (CBD) | 9

intimate and enticing back-street little restaurant beloved of all who dine here. Its patrons come back time and time again, drawn by its dark timber panelling, little tables with little lamps on them, the mood lighting, white tablecloths and, of course, the waiters with the seductive French accents. There are some old French favourites here, such as onion soup and duck terrine, as well as some more unusual versions of roast lamb and chicken with mustard sauce.

The European

161 Spring St, City
✆ 03-9654 0811
🚋 Free city circle tram to Parliament House or tram to top of Bourke St or train to Parliament House Station
Open: daily 0700–2300, The Supper Club even later
Reservations recommended
All credit cards accepted
European
$ $

Serving only European wines (at the last count there were 250 on the wine list), playing European music, and serving only provincial or rustic Italian and French classical food, the concept could be a pretentious disaster in laid-back Melbourne. Yet it works, and works marvellously – this cosy place with the antique bar is always just nicely crowded, whether it be for an early breakfast of croissants and coffee, a lunch of pasta or paella, or a dinner of coq au vin. **The Supper Club** upstairs, with its comfortable lounges, wines and brandy, is so popular with the intellectual 30- to 40-something late-night crowd that it means The European is active almost from dawn to dawn.

The European Grill (EG)

225 King St, City
✆ 03-9642 0102
🚋 Tram up Bourke St to Kingsway or free city circle tram to corner of Spencer St and Lonsdale St or train to Flagstaff Gardens
Open: lunch Mon–Fri from 1200, dinner Thu–Sat from 1700
Reservations unnecessary
All credit cards accepted
Modern Australian
$ $

A popular haunt for lawyers and journalists, EG has a welcoming bar, extensive wine list with many wines by the glass, and a special low-priced *tapas* bar menu, as well as bright and interesting food in its more formal restaurant that has touches of Italian, European and Australian modern trends.

Italy 1

27 George Parade, City
✆ 03-9654 4430
🚋 Tram up Collins St to Russell St
Open: Mon–Sat 0900–late, Sun 1000–late
Reservations recommended
All credit cards accepted
Italian
$ $

If looking for a romantic night, it is worth the effort to find Italy 1, tucked in a back alleyway off Collins St behind the Hyatt Hotel. Small and cramped, with dark timber tables lit only by little lamps, the food here is as good as the atmosphere. The emphasis is on quality, with beautiful tender meat cuts, softly cooked calamari and tiramisu that the waiter claims to be Melbourne's best.

Kuni's ❼

56 Little Bourke St, City
✆ 03-9663 7243
🚋 Tram up Bourke St to Exhibition St
Open: lunch Mon–Fri 1200–2230; dinner Mon–Thu 1800–2200, Fri–Sat 1800–2300
Reservations recommended
All credit cards accepted
Japanese
$ $

With its light pine tables, high ceilings, white walls and staff in blue kimonos, there is a feeling of space and calm as soon as one enters Kuni's. But this is no stuffy *tatami* mat and private room Japanese restaurant; instead, it serves simple good food such as *soba* and *udon* noodles, *tempura*, sushi and *sukiyaki* dishes quickly, efficiently and well.

10 | Central City (CBD)

Madam Fang

27 Crossley St, City

✆ 03-9663 3199

🚋 Free city circle tram to intersection of Spring St with Collins St or tram east up Collins St or train to Parliament House Station

Open: lunch Mon–Fri 1200–1500, dinner Mon–Sat 1800–2300

Reservations recommended

All credit cards accepted

International fusion

$ $

This restaurant sounds Chinese from its name and location near Little Bourke St's Chinatown, but is more like a magpie that has accumulated favourite dishes from around the world. Good value and always vibrant, Madam Fang serves hearty paellas from Spain alongside raw salmon wrapped in *bok choi*.

Marchetti's Latin

55 Lonsdale St, City

✆ 03-9662 1985

🚋 Free city circle tram to Lonsdale St on Spring St or train to Parliament House Station

Open: lunch Sun–Fri 1200–1500; dinner daily 1800–2300

Reservations essential

All credit cards accepted

Italian

$ $ $

This is one of the most prestigious restaurants in Melbourne, an urbane place where the rich and famous brush shoulders with the Establishment, the

▲ Marchetti's Latin

corporate captains and the old Italian families. The food is classical high-class Italian, with plenty of specials such as chilli-flavoured or squid-ink angel-hair pasta, egg *linguine* with truffles and *scaloppine* with forest mushrooms.

Marchetti Tuscan Grill

401 Little Bourke St, City

✆ 03-9670 6612

🚋 Tram along Elizabeth St to Bourke St or up Bourke St to Queen St or underground loop train to Flagstaff Gardens

Open: lunch Mon–Fri 1200–2230, dinner Tue–Sat 0600–2130

Reservations recommended

All credit cards accepted

Italian regional

$ $

Here are the hills of Tuscany painted on the walls, with your table set out in front with a seemingly stunning view. The only problem is the lawyers and barristers who are celebrating their latest win at the table next door. The food is northern Italian, from risottos

and *pappardelle* to traditional Florence grills of beef steak.

Le Restaurant

Level 35 Hotel Sofitel, 25 Collins St, City

✆ 03-9653 0000

🚋 Free city circle tram to the intersection of Spring St with Collins St or tram east up Collins St or train to Parliament House Station

Open: Tue–Sat from 1900

Reservations essential

All credit cards accepted

Modern Australian

$ $ $

Setting out to be one of the highest-class restaurants in town, it succeeds on account of both its fine, although sometimes overly fussy, food and comprehensive wine list, not to mention its spectacular location alongside spacious windows giving a magnificent view from high above the city's buildings.

Shark Fin Inn

50–2 Little Bourke St, City

✆ 03-9662 2681

🚋 Tram up Bourke St to Exhibition St

Central City (CBD) | 11

▲ Chinatown

Open: lunch/yum cha Mon–Fri 1200–1500, Sat 1130–1500, Sun 1100– 1500; dinner daily 1730– 0130

Reservations unnecessary for dinner but essential for weekend yum cha

All credit cards accepted

Chinese

$ $

Located in the heart of bustling Chinatown, Shark Fin Inn is an efficient and unpretentious large restaurant, always packed with Chinese families at enormous round tables. Shark fin soup is naturally the speciality, but must be ordered a day in advance. Otherwise, the fresh seafood combination dishes, stuffed crab claws and prawn dishes are always popular, while its weekend *yum chas* are amongst the town's busiest and best value.

Il Solito Posto ⑬

Basement, 113 Collins St, City; enter via George Parade

✆ 03-9654 4466

🚊 Tram up Collins St to Russell St

Open: Mon–Fri 0700–0100, Sat 0900–0100

Reservations not allowed

All credit cards accepted

Italian

$ $

Located in a narrow alleyway, down a few steps, this is one of Melbourne's secrets, with its polished floors, bookshelves and industrial plumbing throughout. The bar and bistro serve pastas, risottos and salads, all with a great deal of Italian energy and verve, while the cellar restaurant at the back diversifies into *ossobuco*, calamari, rolled lamb with pesto and homemade *linguine* with clams.

Stella ⑭

159 Spring St, City

✆ 03-9639 1555

🚊 Free city circle tram to Parliament House or tram to top of Bourke St or train to Parliament House Station

Open: lunch Mon–Fri 1200–1500, dinner Mon–Sat 1800–2300, supper Mon–Sat from 2230

Reservations recommended

All credit cards accepted

Modern Australian

$ $

Stella is a small, narrow but warm restaurant, with desert-red walls and brightly coloured cushions strewn around its wall bench seats. But food is taken seriously here, even if the atmosphere is more informal than elsewhere, with creative combinations of French, British and Asian touches combined with fresh Australian products. Fish and shellfish are done extremely well; there is often an offal, sausage or pork special. Stella's desserts are justifiably famous and make a great after-show end to the evening.

Sud ⑮

219 King St, City

✆ 03-9670 8451

🚊 Tram up Bourke St to Kingsway or free city circle tram to corner of Spencer St and Lonsdale St or train to Flagstaff Gardens

Open: Mon–Fri 1200–1600, 1800–late

Reservations recommended

All credit cards accepted

Southern Italian

$ $

This is a tiny, narrow restaurant specialising in southern Italian and Sicilian food. There is no relying on formality and pretension here – the air is always filled with laughter, bonhomie and good red wine. Fresh daily specials are the best way to order – or even better is to just wave a hand at owner Umberto Lallo, and ask him to feed you with whatever he thinks is best today.

CENTRAL CITY (CBD)
Bars, cafés and pubs

Arrivederci Aroma [16]
408 Queen St
☏ 03-9606 0530

Try this modern Italian café-bar opposite the Queen Victoria Market, which serves an excellent coffee and Italian food, but in surroundings that are all stainless steel, mirrors and black furniture.

Café Segovia [17]
33 Block Pl.
☏ 03-9650 2373

For a bit of charm, even European sophistication, drop into Café Segovia, which has its big windows opening on to the magic of Block Arcade, while inside there is a sense of privacy and peace for its loyal coffee-set followers.

Campari's [18]
25 Hardware La.
☏ 03-9670 3813

In the midst of little pedestrian Hardware Lane with all its footpath cafés is Campari's, a timeless Italian bistro filled with regulars, most of whom either know their favourite pasta or just load their plate with daily specials straight from the kitchen display.

Gin Palace [19]
190 Little Collins St
☏ 03-9654 0533

Check out the slinky, sophisticated Gin Palace with its Manhattan décor, purple couches, long drapes and killer martinis.

Hairy Canary [20]
212 Little Collins St
☏ 03-9654 2471

To follow the young in-crowd pop into Hairy Canary, with its small space, great pizzas, loud music and wonderful cocktails.

Hopetoun Tea Rooms [21]
Corner of Block Arcade and 282 Collins St
☏ 03-9650 2777

The century-old tearooms are an old favourite, where some of the old ladies still wear hats and white gloves, and where afternoon tea is a must.

Italian Waiters Club [22]
1st floor, 20 Meyers Pl.
☏ 03-9650 1508

Full of noise and fun is the Italian Waiters Club,

▲ Café Segovia

Central City (CBD) | 13

an old haunt of the city's card-playing Italian waiters that now serves hearty and cheap Italian family food.

Kitten Club

Level 2, 267 Little Collins St
✆ 03-9650 2448

This place is supposedly the best chic party venue in town with its faux 1950s décor, purple ceilings, lime-green sofas, padded yellow stools, jazz music and list of more than 100 cocktails.

Kri Kri

39 Little Bourke St
✆ 03-9639 3444

An informal but stylish Greek restaurant with big windows for people-watching and a menu made up entirely of plenty of small dishes to share.

The Lounge

First floor, 243 Swanston St
✆ 03-9663 2916

With its massive balcony, red walls and laid-back feel, The Lounge caters for a mixed casual crowd from university students to groovy office workers.

Meyers Place

20 Meyers Pl., off Bourke St
✆ 03-9650 8609

A favourite bar for the professional crowd – at least on warm summer nights – is the tiny hole-in-the-wall Meyers Place, serving only a few basic spirits, wines and beer, but plenty of lively conversation.

Nudel Bar

76 Bourke St
✆ 03-9662 9100

You can sit at a crowded table and eat noodles from around the world at almost any time of day or night in this great little eatery.

Pellegrini's

66 Bourke St
✆ 03-9662 1885

The best place to start the day is Pellegrini's, an authentic Italian café bar that is a Melbourne institution, serving strong good coffees, Italian cakes, and 1950s-style cheap Italian food around its timber bar, all with plenty of Italian shouting and verve.

Piccolo

Scott Alley, 241 Flinders La.
✆ 03-9654 4999

One of the smallest cafés in town is Piccolo, with its bagels for breakfast and curved timber bar and reputation as the smallest licensed premises in town.

Punch Lane Wine Bar ⑫

43 Little Bourke St
✆ 03-9639 4944

This magnificent bar boasts a broad wine list and pungent cheeses. With wines crowded into racks around the room and its red leather armchairs, it feels like a private club. After shows, many of the fortysomething set move on to **The Supper Club** (see page 10) for a touch of late-night class, fine wines, jazz and classical music.

Tokio ㉙

The Causeway
✆ 03-9650 4144

In the back lane off Bourke St Mall is Tokio, a walk-in Japanese bar where you can either eat or take away excellent and cheap sushi, noodles and lunch boxes.

CENTRAL CITY (CBD)
Shops, markets and picnic sites

Shops

Becco Food Store ❷

11 Crossley St, City
✆ 03-9663 3000
Open: Mon–Sat 0830–2300, Sun 1200–2300

A produce shop which stocks beautiful Italian ingredients, local cheeses, ready-prepared pasta meals, sacks of coffee beans and fruit and vegetables.

Daimaru Food Hall ㉚

Lower ground floor, 211 La Trobe St
✆ 03-9660 6666
Open: Mon–Thu 1000–1800, Fri 1000–2100, Sat 1000–1800, Sun 1100–1800

Pride of place is given to this store's Japanese section, with a large range of soya, *wasabi*, seaweed, noodles, *dashi* and *miso* products, as well as tuna for *sashimi* and beef for *sukiyaki*.

David Jones' Food Glorious Food Hall ㉛

Lower ground floor, Bourke St Mall
✆ 03-9669 8200
Open: Mon–Thu 0900–1800, Fri 0900–2100, Sat 0900–1800 and Sun 1100–1700

This is probably the most extensive food hall in town and it stocks an amazing variety of Australia's best fresh and homemade produce. It might not be the cheapest place to buy food, but this is where you will find meats, seafood, fresh fruit and vegetables, cakes, cheeses, flowers, wine and preserves.

Great Eastern Food Centre ㉜

232 Little Bourke St
✆ 03-9663 3716

You'll find every type of Asian product imaginable here, from noodles and woks to abalone, tofu and black beans.

Haigh's Chocolates ㉑

Shop 26, Block Arcade and 26 Collins St
✆ 03-9654 7673 and 03-9650 2114

For the ultimate shoppers' indulgence, drop into Haigh's Chocolates for its special famous fruit-centred chocolates, or to buy its oh-so-Australian chocolate Easter bilbys.

Maxim's Cakes ㉝

173 Little Bourke St
✆ 03-9662 1980

Snack on divine Asian and Indo-Chinese pastries and cakes, from egg tarts and coconut buns to chocolate mousse cakes and buns filled with red bean paste.

Myer Food Hall ㉞

Ground floor, 295 Lonsdale St
✆ 03-9661 1111
Open: Mon–Wed 1000–1800, Thu 1000–1900, Fri 1000–2100, Sat–Sun 1000–1800

This store has a quick, pick-it-up-on-your-way-home feel, and reasonable prices too. Highlights are its cake section, its takeaway food court and its extensive sweets section.

▲ Becco Food Store

Grand Melbourne dining

The architecture of cooking

Melbourne is often cited by architects and historians as containing some of the best examples of imposing Victorian buildings in the world. Together with its reputation as the culinary capital of Australia, it has made for some magnificent combinations of grand dining with grand settings – the perfect backdrop for that special occasion dinner or celebratory event.

The Grand Dame of Melbourne's formal restaurants is the **Grossi Florentino** (*80 Bourke St, City; ✆ 03-9662 1811; ⓟ trams along Bourke St or underground loop train to Parliament House Station; open: lunch Mon–Fri 1200–1500, dinner Mon–Sat 1800–2300; reservations essential; all credit cards accepted; Grand Italian; ❸❸❸*) set in the shadow of the solid and historic Parliament House. The Florentino has been a Melbourne dining institution for nearly a century. Starting as the Colonial Wine Shop in 1900, in 1926 it was bought by one of Melbourne's leading Italian families, the Massonis from Lucca near Florence, and became an integral part of the social fabric of Melbournes upper echelons.

Its walls are painted by renowned artist Napier Waller, with nine large, colourful mural panels depicting the grandeur and culture of Florentine life: the grand Mural Room dining room has been the setting for many of Melbourne's biggest deals, political intrigues, society scandals and romantic interludes.

But Florentino's is not famous just for its grand surroundings. Its Italian food has always been at the cutting edge of new trends and styles, while the service is exemplary. Old favourites include the suckling lamb cooked in white wine, olive oil and garlic and, of course, Florentino's signature chocolate soufflés. New dishes, such as tortellini of shredded duck and wild mushrooms, or pot-roasted quails with polenta, are proving a real hit with regulars and new diners alike.

> ... the setting for many of Melbourne's biggest deals, political intrigues, society scandals and romantic interludes ...

Just around the corner from the Florentino in Spring St is another marvellous Melbourne old lady, the ornate **Windsor Hotel Grand Ballroom** (*103 Spring St, City; ✆ 03-9633 6000; ⓟ free circular tram along Spring St or trams to top of Bourke and Collins Sts or underground loop train to Parliament House Station; open:*

▲ Windsor Hotel Grand Ballroom

lunch Fri 1200-1430, brunch last Sunday of the month 1130-1500; reservations essential; all credit cards accepted; Modern British; ❸❸) of the roaring boom-time 1880s. Besides being the city's most stately and gracious hotel, its ground-floor Grand Ballroom is one of the grandest dining rooms in town. At the Friday buffet gilt sideboards laden with roast meats, meat platters and fish dishes, all served and presented in the Windsor's modern British style, rest alongside wondrous desserts and cheese platters, while tables groan with elegant, and frequently used, wineglasses. Sunday brunch attracts another dining crowd; here families celebrating special birthdays mingle with romantic couples and overseas visitors. The food choices are endless and beautifully cooked – the problem lies in knowing what to choose. Eggs Benedict, Florentine, scrambled and poached are all available, along with sausages, bacon and mushrooms. But even more tempting are the platters piled high with fresh oysters and prawns, smoked salmon from Tasmania, trout gravadlax and chicken liver pâtés, that never seem to run out. A full roast carvery offering turkey, lamb, tender beef and pork comes next, then there is the wondrous poached barramundi, not to mention the cakes and desserts.

Away from the centre of the city, in suburban Windsor sits the grand Victorian mansion housing another of Melbourne's peerless dining institutions, **Jacques Reymond** (*78 Williams Rd, Windsor; ✆ 03-9525 2178;* ⓟ *trams along High St or suburban train on Sandringham line to Windsor Station; open: lunch Tue-Fri 1200-1400, dinner Tue-Sat 1830-late; reservations essential; all credit cards accepted; Modern French-Australian;* ❸❸❸). Named after its perfectionist host and chef, this restaurant is regularly classed as Melbourne's best, opulent and most classical, both in setting and cuisine style. It is also Melbourne's most expensive restaurant, but food critics rate its food as worth every cent of the experience and taste sensation. Here every attention is paid to detail, the menu is constantly changing, food is impeccably fresh, of the highest quality and beautifully presented, and the faultless dishes are creative and complex, mixing all the best of modern French, European and Australian cooking with Asian touches. Don't miss this grand dining experience.

Southbank

Southbank is the thriving area on the opposite side of the Yarra River from Melbourne's Central City. A small strip of modern restaurants, cafés, shops and entertainment venues based around the three-storey Southgate centre and the Crown casino and entertainment complex, this precinct has grown since the late 1980s to become one of the hubs of cultural and culinary life in the city.

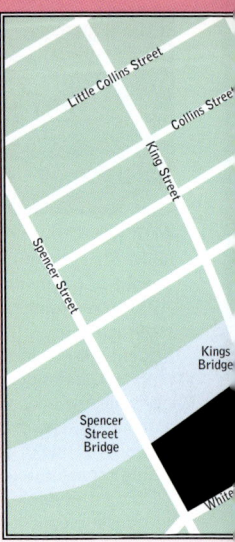

SOUTHBANK
Restaurants

Akvavit ❶

Ground level, Southgate

✆ 03-9699 9947

⦿ Walk from the city centre across Yarra footbridge or take a train to Flinders St Station or a tram along St Kilda Rd to Victorian Arts Centre

Open: daily 1200–1500; Fri-Sat 1800–2400, Sun-Thu 1800–2300

Reservations recommended

All credit cards accepted

Swedish

$$

Akvavit is Melbourne's only Swedish restaurant, and for five years has been instructing Melburnians – as well as hoards of visiting homesick Scandinavians – about the finer points of Nordic cuisine. Akvavit's chefs have shown there is much more to food in Sweden than cheese, cold meats and pickled herring. National favourites include grandma's meatballs and the *sill-bricka* (three types of pickled herring).

Bistro Vite ❶

Shop 2, ground level, Southgate

✆ 03-9690 9271

⦿ Walk from the city centre across Yarra footbridge or take a train to Flinders St Station or tram along St Kilda Rd to Victorian Arts Centre

Open: daily 1200–1500; Fri-Sat 1800–2400, Sun-Thu 1800–2230

Reservations recommended

All credit cards accepted

French

$$

18 | Southbank

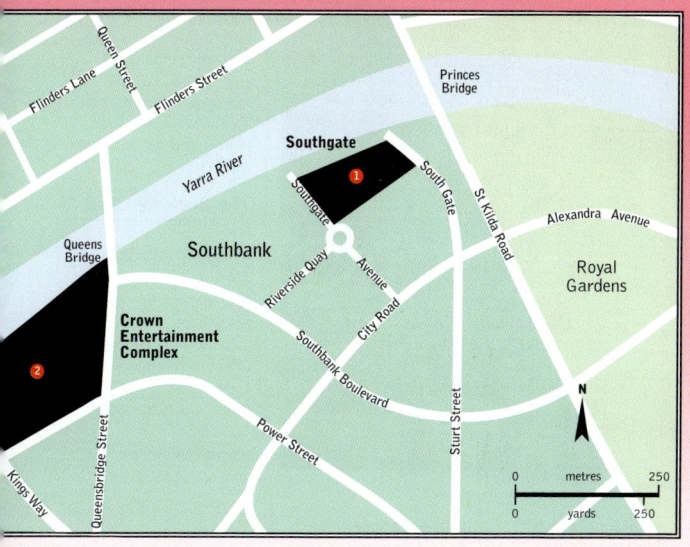

This is a great, buzzing little restaurant to pop into before a spectacular show at the Arts Centre or just to enjoy a chatty lunch or cosy dinner with friends. The food style is not heavy French, but more modern casual bistro fare, although the roast duck and house speciality of *bouillabaisse* would thoroughly warm any French hearts, as would the fresh bread and classic chocolate mousse and crème brûlée desserts.

Blakes ❶

Ground level, Southgate
✆ 03-9699 4100

◉ Walk from the city centre across Yarra footbridge or take a train to Flinders St Station or tram along St Kilda Rd to Victorian Arts Centre

Open: daily 1200–1500, 1800–2300

Reservations essential

All credit cards accepted

Modern Australian

❺❺

Blakes has always stood head and shoulders above the rest for its sheer professionalism mixed with exciting food combining a range of Mediterranean, Asian and Pacific flavours. It is not the cheapest in town and tends towards formality, but is always popular with the corporate crowd, especially when the sun is out and lunch on the blue stone terrace by the river and walking bridge looks inviting. Seafood is cooked especially well here – try the Moreton Bay *bug* and *pomelo* salad or steamed coral trout.

Breezes ❷

Level 3, Crown Entertainment Complex
✆ 03-9292 6896

◉ Walk from the city centre across Queensbridge or take a tram along Spencer St to Crown Entertainment Complex

Open: Mon–Sat 1200–2230, Sun 0730–2230

Reservations recommended

▲ Breezes

All credit cards accepted
Modern Australian
$$

To get to Breezes take the lift to the Crown Towers Hotel and then walk past the Roman-bath like swimming pool and spa. It all makes for a feeling of wellbeing and luxury, even before the magnificent panoramic vista looking out over the Yarra River and the city centre is encountered. The menu is based around a selection of fresh, Mediterranean-inspired dishes, such as *pappardelle* pasta with duck, marinated salmon with a citrus salsa or veal with noodles.

Cecconi's

Ground level, Crown Entertainment Complex
✆ 03-9292 6887
Walk from the city centre across Queensbridge or take a tram along Spencer St to Crown Entertainment Complex
Open: lunch Sun–Fri 1200–1500, dinner daily 1800–late
Reservations recommended
All credit cards accepted
Italian
$$

Cecconi's is a magnificent and vast Italian restaurant that features high ceilings, light décor, expansive windows and a lovely terrace opening on to the walkway beside the Yarra River. This is classy Italian dining – you walk into Cecconi's and instantly feel welcome, relaxed and in a good humour, be it for a business luncheon or a family birthday party. Run by the Italian Bortolotto family, the Italian fare is imaginative, with chic pastas and risottos being followed on the menu by excellent *ossobuco*, rabbit, and other Italian classics.

The Duck

Ground level, Crown Entertainment Complex
✆ 03-9696 5432
Walk from the city centre across Queensbridge or take a tram along Spencer St to Crown Entertainment Complex
Open: daily 1200–1500, 1800–late
Reservations recommended
All credit cards accepted
Modern Australian
$$

Owned by one of Melbourne's leading wine merchants, The Duck is a posh restaurant aimed at a business and gourmet clientele, for whom fine food and exceptional wines are standard essentials of life. A narrow restaurant leading to the waterfront, its décor is business-like and discreet; its menu specialises in several duck options, all accompanied by suggested Pinot Noir wine choices. But the seafood is also cooked well, with modern touches and sauces, while there are some game and kangaroo choices too.

E Gusto

Shop 3B, ground level, Southgate

✆ 03-9690 9819
Walk from the city centre across Yarra footbridge or take a train to Flinders St Station or tram along St Kilda Rd to Victorian Arts Centre

Open: daily 0700–2230
Reservations recommended
All credit cards accepted
Italian
❷❷

Great Italian aromas of garlic and olive oil waft seductively from this riverside quay restaurant, which is one of the few restaurants at Southgate always to open for breakfast. But with its large outdoor eating space, white linen tablecloths, garrulous waiters and general noisy hubbub, E Gusto is a popular lunch and dinner spot, especially with groups of friends. The service can be lax, but the quality of its stylish risottos and pasta dishes keeps the crowds coming back.

Koko

Level 3, Crown Entertainment Complex
✆ 03-9292 6886
Walk from the city centre across Queensbridge or take a tram along Spencer St to Crown Entertainment Complex

Open: lunch daily 1200–1500, dinner Fri–Sat 1800–2400, Sun–Thu 1830–2230
Reservations recommended
All credit cards accepted
Japanese
❷❷

Koko is Melbourne's most exclusive – and expensive – Japanese restaurant. The ambience is instantly calming with its Japanese water garden pool in the centre, dark wooden beams and private *tatami* mat rooms, many with a lovely view across the river to the city skyline. As would be expected, the sushi and *sashimi* are exceptional, and thinly sliced duck, tuna belly and octopus are other delicacies.

Lucky Chan

Shop 42, ground level, Crown Entertainment Complex
✆ 03-9696 3966
Walk from the city centre across Queensbridge or take a tram along Spencer St to Crown Entertainment Complex

Open: daily 1100–2300
Reservations unnecessary
All credit cards accepted
Chinese-Seafood
❷❷

Chinese food is cooked to perfection at Lucky Chan. With many of its tables outside looking over the river and the city, it was a wise choice to focus on Chinese cooking with a seafood emphasis here. Many of the diners are Asian families and businessmen (always a good sign), while specialities include ginger scallops and its ever-popular *yum cha* lunch.

mecca

Mid-level, Southgate
✆ 03-9682 2999
Walk from the city centre across Yarra footbridge or take a train to Flinders St Station or tram along St Kilda Rd to Victorian Arts Centre

Open: daily 1200–1500, 1800–late
Reservations recommended
All credit cards accepted
Middle Eastern-Mediterranean
❷❷

Mecca combines Middle-Eastern and Mediterranean influences with modern Australian cooking. That might sound like a jumble, but the food is superb, from the traditional mecca *meze* with its selection of dips and nibbles, to fish, salads and lamb served with touches such as Turkish eggplant, couscous, tangy lemon flavours, olives and spices.

Red Emperor

Upper level, Southgate
✆ 03-9699 4170
Walk from the city centre across Yarra footbridge or take a train to Flinders St Station or tram along St Kilda Rd to Victorian Arts Centre

Open: lunch Mon–Sat 1200–1500, Sun 1100–1600; dinner daily 1800–2400
Reservations recommended
All credit cards accepted
Chinese
❷❷

With a grand sense of occasion, Red Emperor

serves excellent seafood, tea-smoked Peking duck, and wonderful dumplings. Its *yum cha* lunches are among the best in Melbourne, but make sure you book ahead for the popular Sunday *yum cha* feast.

Ristorante Strega ❷

Shop 10 middle area, ground level, Crown Entertainment Complex

☎ 03-9645 5400

🚇 Walk from the city centre across Queensbridge or take a tram along Spencer St to Crown Entertainment Complex

Open: daily 1200–1500, 1800–2300

Reservations recommended

All credit cards accepted

Italian

$ $

Strega means 'the witch' in Italian and there are few diners who don't fall under its spell after enjoying a quiet, intimate and luxurious Italian meal at this relative newcomer to the Crown restaurant scene. Run by an experienced Italian family of restaurateurs, Strega is a place to linger over magnificently cooked main courses or a light *gnocchi* lunch, all offered with an excellent range of Italian wines.

The River Seafood Bar and Grill ❶

Mid-level, Southgate

☎ 03-9690 4699

🚇 Walk from the city centre across Yarra footbridge or take a train to Flinders St Station or a tram along St Kilda Rd to Victorian Arts Centre

Open: daily 1130–late

Reservations recommended

All credit cards accepted

Seafood

$ $

For a long time Southgate lacked a good seafood restaurant, but fortunately The River stepped in to fill the breach, with its loaded seafood platters at both lunch and dinner weighed down with fresh prawns, oysters, mussels and fish. Serving a mainly business clientele at lunch, the seafood is fresh and plentiful, the wines fine and the timber bar is great to perch at for a drink even without eating a full meal.

Scusa Mi ❶

Mid-level, Southgate

☎ 03-9699 4111

🚇 Walk from the city centre across Yarra footbridge or take a train to Flinders St Station or a tram along St Kilda Rd to Victorian Arts Centre

Open: lunch Mon–Fri 1200–1430, Sat–Sun 1200–1500; dinner daily 1800–2230

Reservations always recommended and essential at weekends

All credit cards accepted

Italian

$ $ $

This is a pricey, sophisticated restaurant in the most perfect of Southgate locations, with its long balcony overlooking the Yarra River and the entrancing city skyline and night lights. But the restaurant prides itself on showcasing all that is best about modern Italian cuisine, and uses only the finest ingredients, while chef Simon Humble recently won a chef's competition in Italy as the best risotto cook outside the homeland. The signature dish of roast duckling in an Aperol and orange sauce should never be refused.

Waterfront ❷

Shop 19, Ground level, Crown Entertainment Complex

☎ 03-9686 9744

🚇 Walk from the city centre across Queensbridge or take a tram along Spencer St to Crown Entertainment Complex

Open: daily 1200–1600, 1800–2300

Reservations not allowed

All credit cards accepted

Seafood

$ $

A dazzling display of fresh seafood at the entrance to this busy restaurant entices passers-by and visiting Asian tourists. This is a great place for quick dining with a group of friends, or a long celebratory dinner over the heaped seafood platters. Food is fairly standard fresh seafood dishes, although the flounder *meunière* is a great favourite.

SOUTHBANK
Bars, cafés and pubs

Automatic Café

Shop 30/31, ground floor, Crown Entertainment Complex
✆ 03-9690 2229

Always full and bopping is the retro Automatic Café which features coloured laminate tables and chairs, opens out on to the river terrace, and serves casual pizza, stir-fries, pastas and burgers in one of the best-value and cheerful atmospheres in town.

Blue Train Café ❶

Mid-level, Southgate
✆ 03-9696 0111

The Blue Train Café aims at a younger set more interested in unpretentious food such as wood-fired pizzas and wok-tossed stir-fries, all costing less than a fine glass of wine. It's noisy, it's busy, and you can't book, but the Blue Train is always full, whether for breakfast, coffee, lunch, dinner or a late-night snack in its groovy retro lounge.

Brubakers Bagel Bar ❷

Ground floor, Crown Entertainment Complex
✆ 03-9686 2200

This place opens from 0800 and sells the best bagels in town. Coffee and all-round breakfast here is hard to beat too.

Cervo Café

Shop 28, ground floor, Crown Entertainment Complex
✆ 03-9292 7824

For a touch more Italian than New York flavour, Cervo Café opens from 1100 until late into the night, specialising in its strong coffees and Italian trattoria-style lunches and dinners.

The Deck Café ❶

Middle level, Southgate
✆ 03-9699 9544

This café specialises in great breakfasts from 0730, especially for the power-breakfast working set who like to sit on its open-air terrace with their laptops and eggs Florentine. It also serves some of the best, and cheapest, coffee in Southbank.

Fidel's Cigar Bar

Level B1, Crown Entertainment Complex
✆ 03-9292 6885

The intriguing Fidel's Cigar Bar, with its deep leather armchairs, cognacs and Cuban cigars, is ideal for a stylish late-night drink away from the beat of the nightclubs or jangle of the gambling rooms. Featuring a full range of exotic beers, liqueurs and wines, as well as boxes of cigars all longer than your arm, this is an impressive bar, although not one well suited to the anti-smoking brigade.

Pasta Express

Shop 103, level 1, Crown Entertainment Complex
✆ 03-9696 8884

▲ Fidel's Cigar Bar

▲ Simply French

This quick and buzzing budget café serves cheap *gnocchi*, cannelloni, spaghetti and pizza by the slice for those wanting a grab-it-'n'-run feed.

Rhumba's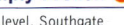

Ground level, Southgate
✆ 03-9696 2973

Ultra-casual Rhumba's is the only licensed café in the food court and serves light meals from 0900 until 2300, all ordered from behind the bar, along with its wine bottles and wine by the glass.

Savi Bar and Café

Middle level, Southgate
✆ 03-9699 3600

The classy Savi Bar and Café opens from noon until midnight and features an extensive wine list from all around Australia and overseas, plus a quick casual bar menu of risottos, fish 'n' chips, dips and burgers, as well as full restaurant service of modern Australian cuisine.

Simply French

Top level, Southgate
✆ 03-9699 9804

This is a popular restaurant and café with its bistro French food and traditions. But it is its separate **Maurice's Wine Bar**, complete with wood panelling, that comes into its own late at night, specialising in French champagne, wines and aged cognac for the cognoscenti.

Walter's Wine Bar

Level 3, Southgate
✆ 03-9690 9211

One of Melbourne's great dining and drinking institutions, Walter's Wine Bar is everything from a thriving café and restaurant, to a late-night wine bar and a home-from-home for many of the performers at the adjacent Victorian Arts Centre. With its swish, clean lines, lovely curved timber bar filled with wine devotees, and views over the city, Walter's has one of the best wine cellars in Melbourne. As well as being a terrific watering-hole, it is a moderately expensive restaurant for a quick bite before the opera or a full-on celebratory meal. Many wines are served by the glass and the bar staff are all wine experts. Great after-show desserts with sticky wines too.

SOUTHBANK
Shops, markets and picnic sites

Shops

Charmaine's Ice Cream

Southgate Food Court
✆ 03-9415 1872

Open daily, this place is a favourite with adults and children alike for its rich ice-cream flavours such as *baci*, chocolate chilli, lemon cheesecake and gingerbread, as well as its classic lime Cointreau sorbet.

Lettuce and Lovage

Southgate Food Court
✆ 03-9699 9959

A vegetarian's delight, this self-serve salad bar sells a variety of salads, hot potatoes, vegetarian soups and vegetable pastries.

The Lolly Box

Southgate Food Court
✆ 03-9699 9961

Here you can delve into more than 40 colours and flavours of jelly beans and jelly babies, as well as every sort of sweet and lolly imaginable.

The Nut Shack

Southgate Food Court
✆ 03-9690 9885

Stocks abound of every type of nut from macadamia and pistachios to hazelnuts, almonds, peanuts and cashew. You can also pick up ginger, fudge, Turkish delight and coffee beans.

Pizzetti

Southgate Food Court
✆ 03-9682 4677

Sells takeaway pastas and pizza by the slice.

Shoji

Southgate Food Court
✆ 03-9699 9980

Indulge in quality takeaway Japanese and Korean food, such as sushi boxes and Korean noodles with *kimchi*.

Walter's Wine and Food Store

Upper level, Southgate
✆ 03-9690 3200

Opposite the famous Walter's Wine Bar (*see page 24*), this store sells a large range of homemade preserves, jams, jellies and pickles, alongside olive oils, vinegars, cheeses, breads, Australian honey and Walter's own ice cream and chocolates. An extensive wine cellar also sells one of the broadest selections of fine wines in town.

Business dining

Dining to impress

Meals mean deals in Melbourne, just as much as in any other business capital of the world. But, with Melbourne's classy, old-European overtones, the emphasis here for business dining is on the quality of the food and the prestige of the restaurant.

Most business deals in Melbourne tend to be negotiated over lunch rather than dinner. The accepted etiquette is that the nitty-gritty of the business transaction is not discussed until the main course is out of the way – often it may not even be mentioned until coffee is on the table.

The ultimate place for a discreet deal-making lunch in Melbourne is the **Flower Drum** Chinese restaurant (*17 Market La., Melbourne city; ✆ 03-9662 3655; ◉ tram along Bourke St to Parliament House; open: lunch Mon–Sat 1200–1500, dinner daily 1800–2200; reservations essential; all credit cards accepted; Chinese; ❸❸❸*). The accolades for the Flower Drum are as much due to its ever-attentive owner, Gilbert Lau, as its exceptional Cantonese food. You can rely on regular new offerings and fresh ingredients flown in from around the globe.

Coincidentally, **Silks** (*level 1, Crown Entertainment Complex, Southbank; ✆ 03-9292 6888; ◉ walk from the city centre across the Yarra footbridge or take a train to Flinders St Station or take the Spencer St tram to the Crown Casino; open: lunch daily 1200–1500, dinner 1800–2400; reservations essential; all credit cards accepted; Chinese; ❸❸❸*), another of Melbourne's most popular business venues, is also an expensive Cantonese restaurant which offers traditional cuisine in the setting of a Chinese mansion, including a magnificent silk Mongolian tent as its centrepiece. Its prices are as over-the-top as its setting, but the views over the Melbourne skyline and the Yarra River are exceptional.

Langton's (*61 Flinders La., City; ✆ 03-9663 0222; ◉ tram along Collins St to Exhibition St; open: lunch Mon–Fri from 1200,*

▲ Silks

dinner Mon–Sat from 1800; reservations essential; all credit cards accepted; Modern French; ❸❸❸) is a newcomer to the Melbourne restaurant scene, but its French master, joint owner and chef, Phillipe Mouchel, is well-known to many Melbourne gourmands already, as is his partner, wine specialist and wine auctioneer, Stewart Langton. Langton's has quickly acquired a loyal following of business, legal and political devotees, who love its dark corners and theatrical air, almost as much as its impressive modern food and exceptional Australian and French wine list. This is the restaurant for a long lunch, accompanied by several bottles of wine, where business deals can be completed or celebrated away from prying eyes.

Caterina's Cucina e Bar (*221 Queen St, City; ✆ 03-9670 8488; 🚋 tram along Bourke St to Queen St; open: lunch Mon–Fri 1200–1500; reservations recommended; all credit cards accepted; Italian;* ❸❸) is another city basement restaurant beloved of lawyers-who-lunch, but the prices here are more moderate than Langton's and the food is Italian. Risottos, roast kid, salmon carpaccio and *polpetto* meatballs are all served with style and the wine list is as good as the legal gossip that frequently circulates within its walls.

Away from the city centre, but close to the advertising businesses and corporate office blocks of St Kilda Rd and South Yarra, is the venerable business lunch favourite of **Lynch's** (*133 Domain Rd, South Yarra; ✆ 03-9866 5627; 🚋 tram to South Yarra along St Kilda Rd and Domain Rd; open: lunch, Mon–Fri 1200–1430, dinner Mon–Sat 1830–2400; reservations essential; all credit cards accepted; International;* ❸❸❸). Adjacent to the Botanic Gardens, Lynch's is an old-world, expensive but classic place to bring an esteemed business partner or associate, with a touch of 19th-century decadence thrown in for good measure. The food is relatively traditional, but always cooked to perfection, the wine list is deep, and the atmosphere is both intimate and discreet.

For a total contrast, when you want to celebrate a business success late at night, flamboyantly and ostentatiously, the place to be seen is **JJ's Champagne Bar and Grill** (*level 1, Crown Entertainment Complex, Southbank; ✆ 03-9292 6891; 🚋 train to Flinders St or tram across Spencer St bridge to Crown Casino; open: daily 1700–0200; reservations unnecessary; all credit cards accepted; International;* ❸❸). Regarded as the deal-making heart of Melbourne's 'New Money' scene, JJ's serves fresh seafood and Victorian beef, as well as innumerable glasses of the best champagne to all those business powerbrokers and people-watchers who pass through its glitzy doors.

> ... a long lunch, accompanied by several bottles of wine, where business deals can be completed or celebrated away from prying eyes ...

St Kilda and Bayside

St Kilda and its bayside suburbs of Port Melbourne, South Melbourne, Middle Park and Albert Park have a happening restaurant, bar and pub-dining scene. Flanking the golden edge of Port Phillip Bay, ringed by beachside palm trees and a roller-blading track, and with the backdrop of the city centre, in this part of Melbourne almost anything goes.

ST KILDA AND BAYSIDE
Restaurants

Bedi's ❶

118 Park St, South Melbourne

☏ 03-9690 8233

🚋 Tram 1 or 12 along Kings Way from City to Park St

Open: lunch Mon–Fri 1200–1430, dinner Mon–Sat 1830–2200

Reservations recommended

All credit cards accepted

Indian

💲💲

This is the home of North Indian and tandoori cooking; a small, busy restaurant surrounded by leafy plane trees, little parks and advertising agencies of South Melbourne. Bedi's serves a wide range of curries and Indian food in casual, no-fuss surroundings, although it is its famous chicken butter cream dish that ensures its continuing popularity.

Café di Stasio ❷

31 Fitzroy St, St Kilda

☏ 03-9525 3999

🚋 St Kilda light-rail tram down Bourke St from the city centre to halfway down Fitzroy St

Open: daily 1200–1500, 1800–2300

Reservations essential

All credit cards accepted

Italian

💲💲

One of the first high-class restaurant arrivals when Fitzroy St was first escaping from its tawdry red-light era, Café di Stasio remains a favourite lunch and dinner spot, with its professional service and simple yet vastly refined Italian cuisine. Dishes include impeccable angel-hair pasta, *saltimbocca*, lamb fillets, carpaccio and great bread. Smoking puts off some diners, but the atmosphere is always jovial, yet elegant.

Circa, the Prince ❸

The Prince of Wales Hotel, 2 Acland St, St Kilda

☏ 03-9536 1122

🚋 St Kilda light-rail tram down Bourke St from the city centre to the end of Fitzroy St

Open: daily 1200–1430, 1830–2230

Reservations essential

All credit cards accepted

Modern European

💲💲💲

The neglected art-deco Prince of Wales Hotel has been re-opened as a grand bar and dining complex containing Melbourne's most theatrical restaurant, Circa. With its voluminous black atmosphere, white linen tablecloths, huge vases of flowers and stylish assortment of eclectic furniture and decorations, the melodrama could easily outweigh its menu. Fortunately the classical food is sublime and the Australian and French wine list magnificent, with the chef blending complex European sauces and modern British touches such as artichokes, pigs' trotters and partridge with magnificent eye fillet, crabs, mussels, fish, veal and duck.

Donovans ❹

40 Jacka Boulevard, St Kilda

☏ 03-9534 8221

🚋 St Kilda light-rail tram down Bourke St from the city centre to close to Acland St and St Kilda Pier

Open: Mon–Fri 1200–2230, Sat–Sun brunch/lunch 1000–1700, dinner 1700–2230

Reservations essential

All credit cards accepted

Modern Australian

💲💲

Another great Melbourne dining experience that is probably closest to a Californian beach-house pavilion in atmosphere. There are soft lounges, throw cushions, fine paintings, a roaring fire in winter and great views of the

▲ The Point

sun setting over the Bay in the evening. The food is bold and amongst Melbourne's best, with the duck, mussels in aniseed broth and blue swimmer crab the star performers in an excellent and enticing menu.

est est est

440 Clarendon St, South Melbourne
✆ 03-9682 5688
🚋 Tram 10, 12, 17 or 96 down Spencer St from the city centre to far end of Clarendon St
Open: Mon–Sat from 1830
Reservations essential
All credit cards accepted
European
$ $

The motto of the award-winning restaurant, est est est, is 'less is more' and – with the exception perhaps of the wine list of more than 400 wines from around the globe – that certainly is the ambience of this white and slightly austere temple to good food. There is no pretension here; the quality of the food and ingredients is simply the best that can be obtained, be it the *foie gras*, truffles, wild mushrooms, crayfish, ravioli of quail or the mouth-watering chocolate soufflé.

Isthmus of Kra

50 Park St, South Melbourne
✆ 03-9690 3688
🚋 Tram along St Kilda Rd from the city centre to the Shrine, and turn right down Park St
Open: Mon–Fri 1200–1500, dinner daily from 1800
Reservations recommended
All credit cards accepted
Nonya Thai
$ $

This up-market Thai restaurant, much admired by corporate executives and neighbouring television station workers, serves a mean red duck curry, delectable 'oysters of passion' with lemongrass dressing and a *tom yum* soup which is second to none. The interior of the restaurant is elegantly Thai, with its brass cutlery and beautiful pottery dishes.

La Madrague

171 Buckhurst St, South Melbourne
✆ 03-9699 9627
🚋 Port Melbourne light-rail tram down Collins St in the city centre to Montague St, Port Melbourne
Open: Mon–Fri 1200–1500, 1900–2200
Reservations recommended
All credit cards accepted
French
$ $

The loyal devotees of this restaurant keep on coming back for the wonderful pepper steak with *frites*, the onion soup, the fresh snails with blue cheese sauce and the *confit* of duck with garlic potatoes. And, of course, its ultra-rich chocolate mousse.

Melbourne Wine Room

The George Hotel, 125 Fitzroy St, St Kilda
✆ 03-9525 5599
🚋 St Kilda light-rail tram down Bourke St from the city centre to the old St Kilda railway station
Open: daily 1830–2300
Reservations recommended
All credit cards accepted
Mediterranean
$ $

This popular restaurant puts as much emphasis on wine as it does on food. The wine waiters here are well informed and their suggestions are usually spot-on. Be it freshly shucked oysters, a whole baby snapper, or the magnificent chargrilled rib-eye of aged beef, you can be sure the ingredients are always of the best quality from specialist suppliers and the wine at the perfect temperature. Desserts are outstanding too, and an after-dinner drink at the front wine bar can turn into a long night of merriment.

Misuzu's

7 Victoria Ave., Albert Park
✆ 03-9699 9022
🚋 Tram 12 down Clarendon St or the St Kilda light-rail tram to Albert Park
Open: daily 1200–1500, 1730–2200
Reservations essential

Japanese

This is a bright little Japanese café that serves food far above the standard sushi rolls on a polystyrene plate. Sit outside in the sun and enjoy excellent and ample servings of tofu, *sashimi*, *sukiyaki*, *udon* noodles and sushi, or upstairs where the food is a little more formal and creative.

Near East

254 Park St, South Melbourne
✆ 03-9699 1900
🚋 Tram 10 or 12 from the city centre, down Spencer St, Clarendon St and into Park St
Open: lunch Mon–Fri 1100–1500, dinner daily 1830–2230
Reservations recommended
All credit cards accepted
South-east Asian

The minute you walk into Near East with its wide windows, timber floors, cathedral ceilings and tasteful brass and bamboo decorations, there is a feeling of space, calm and oriental order. This is a restaurant where the Asian owners and chefs blend tastes and ingredients from a mix of Thai, Malay and Indonesian cooking. The oysters with their little clay pot lids are a must-have starter, while Gulf of Carpentaria prawns and Malaccan whole fish cooked in banana leaves with lime and lemongrass dressing are two other hot favourites.

One Fitzroy St

1 Fitzroy St, St Kilda
✆ 03-9593 8800
🚋 St Kilda light-rail tram down Bourke St from the city centre to the end of Fitzroy St
Open: daily 1200–1500, 1800–2400
Reservations recommended
All credit cards accepted
Modern Australian

This is a stylish restaurant with a dress-circle view of all the St Kilda action from its chrome balcony. Strong on vegetarian offerings such as its Mediterranean vegetable terrine, lasagne with goats' cheese and leek, and spinach and chicory risotto, as well as other modern dishes such as grilled sausage Lyonnaise and a delicious Japanese platter. Service is often erratic, and paying steep prices for extras such as chips and vegetables can be offensive, but the balmy summer breezes, the suntrap veranda and the bobbing yachts compensate.

The Point

Aquatic Dr., Albert Park Lake, Albert Park
✆ 03-9682 5544
🚋 Tram 12 to end of Clarendon St and Albert Park Lake

▲ Near East's food stall at the Melbourne Food and Wine Festival

Open: daily 1200–1500, 1800–late
Reservations recommended
All credit cards accepted
Modern Australian
$$

Sit upstairs and relax in this spacious restaurant with the sweeping glass windows and balcony overlooking Albert Park Lake. The crowd that come here to eat are mainly attractive 'ladies who lunch' and men in dark business suits. The food is a mixture of modern Australian dishes, but using impeccable quality ingredients and with unusual touches to make it stand out well above the ordinary.

Stavros Tavern ⑬

183 Victoria St, Albert Park
☏ 03-9699 5618
🚊 Tram 1 bound for South Melbourne Beach from the city centre down Clarendon St and Victoria Ave
Open: Tue–Sun from 1800
Reservations recommended
All credit cards accepted
Greek
$$

Thousands of Greek migrants arrived at Port Melbourne's Station Pier in the 1960s and 1970s as new Australians, and many ended up settling in the small workers' cottages that dot the shoreline and suburbs of Port Melbourne and South Melbourne. One result has been Stavros Tavern, a bright Greek restaurant that oozes a sense of sun, olives, island harbours and even ouzo. Weekend nights are rowdy with live music, but the food is above ordinary, with regional dishes featuring fish, lamb shanks, homemade Greek sausages, octopus, vegetarian bean stews and even okra.

The Stokehouse ⑭

30 Jacka Boulevard, St Kilda
☏ 03-9525 5555
🚊 St Kilda light-rail tram down Bourke St from the city centre to close to Acland St and St Kilda Pier
Open: upstairs dining room, daily 1200–1500, 1800–2230; downstairs café, Mon–Sat 1100–0100, Sun 1000–0100
Reservations recommended
All credit cards accepted
Modern Australian
$$–$$$

From the outside, The Stokehouse looks like a white yacht club perched right on the beachfront and surrounded by date palm trees. Upstairs is a beautiful open and airy dining room, with whitewashed walls and timber floors, leading on to outside deck dining in summer and with views in all directions over the Bay. It is always buzzing with action, with famous people and with a sense of fun and gaiety. The food is always creative and impeccably presented and served, although The Stokehouse is more about a relaxing night of enjoyable dinner with friends in great surroundings, than akin to worshipping at a gourmand temple. The menu is modern Australian, featuring plenty of fresh seafood, risottos, beef and chicken options.

Tolarno Bar and Bistro ⑮

42 Fitzroy St, St Kilda
☏ 03-9525 5477
🚊 St Kilda light-rail tram down Bourke St from the city centre to the start of Fitzroy St
Open: lunch Sun–Fri 1200–1500, dinner daily 1800–2300
Reservations recommended
All credit cards accepted
Modern Australian
$$

With its brightly coloured painted windows, murals on the walls, and cosy bohemian ambience, Tolarno's is a warm little restaurant to go to for a good dose of comfort food, good red wine and reasonable prices. Behind the bar is TV celebrity chef Iain Hewitson, who is as full-bodied and unpretentious as his restaurant, dishing up his famous bar-burgers, smoked bangers and mash, barbecued Tasmanian salmon and other good-natured fare, while the wine specials on the blackboard are a good place to look for bargains.

ST KILDA AND BAYSIDE
Bars, cafés and pubs

189 Espresso Bar 16

189 Acland St, St Kilda
☎ 03-9534 8884

Enjoy coffee and an upmarket breakfast while sitting with the morning papers on the outside pavement and people-watch to your heart's content.

Bar Corvina 17

157 Fitzroy St, St Kilda
☎ 03-9537 0244

Open from 1000 until 0100, this is a great place for a quiet drink in the dark, a strong coffee or a simple, candlelit meal.

Birdcage 8

George Hotel, 129 Fitzroy St, St Kilda
☎ 03-9534 0277

The narrow foyer bar of this imposing hotel serves 'Japanesque' bits and pieces, from sushi and gravadlax salmon with seaweed dressing to braised eel and crêpes with green tea custard, until late into the night.

Café a taglio 17

157 Fitzroy St, St Kilda
☎ 03-9534 1344

Pizza eating in Melbourne is taken to a new level at this Italian gem, where pizzas with such delectable toppings as gorgonzola and mushroom are sold by the slice (*a taglio*).

Café Barcelona 29

25 Fitzroy St, St Kilda
☎ 03-9525 4244

Tapas-style eating is on offer here, where Spanish flair matches sherries and Spanish wines to each *tapas* enticement.

Café Racer 18

15a/16 Marine Parade, St Kilda
☎ 03-9534 9988

Where the motorbikes line up outside, most of the crowd wear rollerblades or leather jackets and the hectic cycle path zips past on the other side of Marine Parade as the caffeine fix does its early-morning job.

Café Sweethearts 19

263 Coventry St, South Melbourne
☎ 03-9690 6752

Across the road from the bustling South

▲ St Kilda Pier Kiosk

St Kilda and Bayside | 33

▲ Dogs Bar

Melbourne markets, Café Sweethearts is a sunny, yellow-and-blue little cottage that was one of the first breakfast/brunch trendsetters in the area with its fresh orange juice, fruit muesli and eggs Benedict.

Chinta Blues 20

6 Acland St, St Kilda

✆ 03-9534 9233

A cheap Malaysian coffeehouse and hawkers' restaurant filled with good Malay food and blues music.

Cicciolina 30

130 Acland St, St Kilda

✆ 03-9525 3333

For lunch or a late-night meal, Cicciolina's serves tasty Mediterranean specials and unbeatable coffee.

Dogs Bar 31

54 Acland St, St Kilda

✆ 03-9525 3599

Favourite haunt of a quieter, older crowd, who hang out here to experience its exceptional wine list and late-night conversations.

Le Kiosk on the Beach 21

Beaconsfield Parade, near Kerferd Rd intersection

✆ 03-9696 6334

One of the best breakfast spots where the kids can paddle in the sea while their parents enjoy a hearty breakfast in the sun.

Mink Bar 20

2 Acland St, underground bar beneath the Prince of Wales Hotel, St Kilda

✆ 03-9536 1199

The cool Mink Bar has plush velvet seats, champagne, caviar and 43 types of frozen vodka on hand.

Scheherezade Restaurant and Coffee Lounge 32

99 Acland St, St Kilda

✆ 03-9534 2722

A great place for coffee, preferably at Saturday breakfast when all the old Jewish grandfathers come out to play. It is hard to walk past Scheherezade's without stopping to enjoy its hearty Jewish kosher food, Yiddish talk, huge chunks of cheesecake, fried schnitzels, great strong coffees and sense of historic place as the first restaurant in Acland St.

St Kilda Pier Kiosk 22

End of St Kilda Pier

✆ 03-9535 3198

For afternoon tea, or even a light fish 'n' chips lunch, the choice is easy – every visitor to St Kilda must stroll along its pier at least once and eat in the St Kilda Pier Kiosk, while the water laps around, the yachts bob in the marina, the seagulls eat chip remnants from paper wrappers and where the coffee and cake options are surprisingly good.

Victory Café 33

Light-rail Station, 60 Fitzroy St, St Kilda

✆ 03-9534 3727

This is a quiet hang-out for everyone to enjoy breakfast and coffee from families and friends to up-and-coming starlets, while the trams rattle past.

ST KILDA AND BAYSIDE
Shops, markets and picnic sites

Shops

Albert Park Deli ❷❸

129 Dundas Pl., Albert Park

✆ 03-9699 9594

This is the pick of the cafés to nibble and lunch at, as well as stocking a great range of fresh meats and cheeses, and a wealth of take-home pre-cooked meals from beef stroganoff and chicken *cacciatore* to cakes, muffins, tiramisu and warming soups.

Il Fornaio ❷⓿

Prince of Wales Hotel, 2 Acland St, St Kilda

✆ 03-9534 2922

Drop in to Il Fornaio, where every type of bread from sourdough to croissants can be bought, topped off by treats such as profiteroles and lemon tarts.

Montague Park Food Store ❷❹

406 Park St, South Melbourne

✆ 03-9682 9680

You can buy fresh home-cooked baguettes, cakes and a full range of pre-cooked meals, which can be chosen while enjoying a coffee in the sun outside this little corner terrace house.

The Vital Ingredient ❷❺

206 Clarendon St, South Melbourne

✆ 03-9696 3511

Known as the store where the chefs shop, this place is filled to bursting with all the best of every cuisine and culture, from lentils from Le Puy in France, to sherry vinegar from Spain, *verjuice* from Maggie Beer's kitchen, and Australian bush foods from *quandongs* to *bunya bunya* nuts.

Markets

Melbourne Organics ❷❻

219 Ferrars St, South Melbourne

✆ 03-9690 9339

Tantalising, beautifully coloured, organic fruit and vegetables sourced from all around Australia are sold in a large warehouse, alongside a full range of dried organic legumes, grains and cereals.

South Melbourne Market ❷❼

Corner of Coventry St and Cecil St, South Melbourne

✆ 03-9209 6295

Open: Wed 0730–1400, Fri 0730–1800, Sat 0730–1400, Sun 0800–1600

Shopping for food delicacies in the St Kilda and Bayside area almost starts and finishes at the South Melbourne Market. With its full range of delicatessens, Asian food, butchers' shops, seafood stores and bakeries, all housed in stalls under one big pavilion, alongside a good selection of clothing, flower, kitchenware and linen stalls, it is easy to buy the whole dinner party menu or picnic basket ingredients here.

Picnic sites

Albert Park Lake ❷❽

 Tram 12 to end of Clarendon St and Albert Park Lake

In winter, rug up and head for the shores of Albert Park Lake, where the swans and ducks can be fed, football watched on weekends and a brisk walk around the lake enjoyed.

Beaches

On a warm day, just head for the beach and the nearest vacant spot of sand – the beaches from **Port Melbourne** to **Elwood** ❸❹ and beyond are fine for swimming.

St Kilda and Bayside | 35

Melbourne's Bayside pub scene

Transforming history

As befits a city that mushroomed in size following the rich gold rushes of the 1850s and 60s, and relied on sailing ships and the docks for its immigrants and wealth, the Bay and inner riverside suburbs of Melbourne are littered with rip-roaring pubs, bars and hotels. Few remain the dens of iniquity or the hangouts of murderers, bushrangers, runaway sailors and hardened criminals that they once were. Now Melbourne's best pubs, especially those in Port Melbourne, South Melbourne, Middle Park and St Kilda, are more likely to house elegant restaurants, lively wine bars, comedy club venues and regular jazz, rock and music nights.

The **O'Connell Centenary Hotel** (*corner Montague St and Coventry St, South Melbourne; ∅ 03-9699 9600;* ⓠ *light-rail tram to South Melbourne Market; open: bistro lunch daily 1200–1500, dinner daily 1800–2100, restaurant lunch Mon–Fri 1200–1500, dinner Tue–Sat 1900–late; reservations recommended for bistro but essential for restaurant; all credit cards accepted; Modern Mediterranean;* ❸❸) was once a pub for Irish working-class patriots, but has now been transformed into one of Melbourne's culinary landmarks, while still remaining a lively local pub for the area's increasingly trendy young residents. The polished timber front bar and cosy relaxed bistro, as well as the summer outdoor eating area in front of the hotels, serves breezy modern food for lunch and dinner at easily affordable prices.

Just down the road in the main street of Port Melbourne is another corner pub that remains the preserve of Melbourne's booming immigrant Irish and adopted Irish population. Except on St Patrick's Day, when the street outside **Molly Bloom's** (*39 Bay St, Port Melbourne; ∅ 03-9646 2681;* ⓠ *light-rail tram to Port Melbourne from the city centre; open: Mon–Fri lunch 1130–1430, dinner 1730–2100; Sat–Sun 1130–2100; reservations recommended; all credit cards accepted; Irish;* ❸) is filled with young Irish drunks getting 'flootered' on green Guinness, this pub is effortlessly Irish without a gimmick in sight. The bar menu is pretty basic chips-and-Guinness fare, while **Joyce's** restaurant is a great place for a hearty, filling and cheap meal of meat, vegetables and 'tatties', or seafood, pasta and risotto.

Sitting right on the edge of Port Phillip Bay by Station Pier, where so many of Melbourne's immigrants arrived by ship during the 1940s, 50s and 60s, is the up-market **London Hotel** (*92 Beach St, Port Melbourne; ⌀ 03-9646 4644;* 🚋 *light-rail tram to Port Melbourne from the city centre; open: café daily 0700-2200, restaurant lunch Sun-Fri 1200-1500, dinner Tue-Sat 1800-2200; reservations recommended; all credit cards accepted; Modern;* ❸❸). Once a rough sailors' pub, the London has now been embraced by the chic new Bayside apartment and housing precinct of Beacon Cove, and the hotel has changed its stripes accordingly. Upstairs is an excellent, if pricey restaurant, where the minimalist white walls and light timber floors turn the eyes outwards to the Bay with its ships and yachts. The food here is modern, creative and elegant, with a good emphasis on beautifully prepared seafood and a wide range of vegetarian dishes. Downstairs the café-bar is a popular meeting and drop-in spot, whether as a place to enjoy a leisurely quiet breakfast with the Sunday papers, a light lunch with friends, or a cool glass of wine and simple romantic dinner on a balmy summer's evening.

The food at **Swallows** (*192 Station St, Port Melbourne; ⌀ 03-9646 2746;* 🚋 *light-rail tram to Port Melbourne from the city centre; open: Sun-Fri lunch 1200-1430, daily dinner 1800-2100; reservations unnecessary; all credit cards accepted; Modern;* ❸❸) is focused on good ingredients, the dining room is

▲ Molly Bloom's

cosy and intimate, the owner has imbued the hotel with his own style, and fine wines for sampling are always on hand. The special wine dinners, or Sunday music nights, are not to be missed; equally delightful are the fresh French cheeses and the *pétanque* (*bocce*) playing square outside in the park for the pleasure of the Swallows' patrons.

> *... the minimalist white walls and light timber floors turn the eyes outwards to the Bay with its ships and yachts ...*

For a completely different scene, try **The George Hotel** (*125 Fitzroy St, St Kilda; ⌀ 03-9525 5599;* 🚋 *light-rail tram to St Kilda from the city centre; open: daily 1200-2300, later at weekends; reservations unnecessary; all credit cards accepted; Modern;* ❸❸) in St Kilda's bustling main street. A grand three-storey edifice, The George has been an 'in' place for the young, trendy, black-garbed set for the past six years, ever since its owner progressively opened up rooms in the previously derelict grand old hotel for wine bars, restaurants, café-bakeries and even several art cinemas.

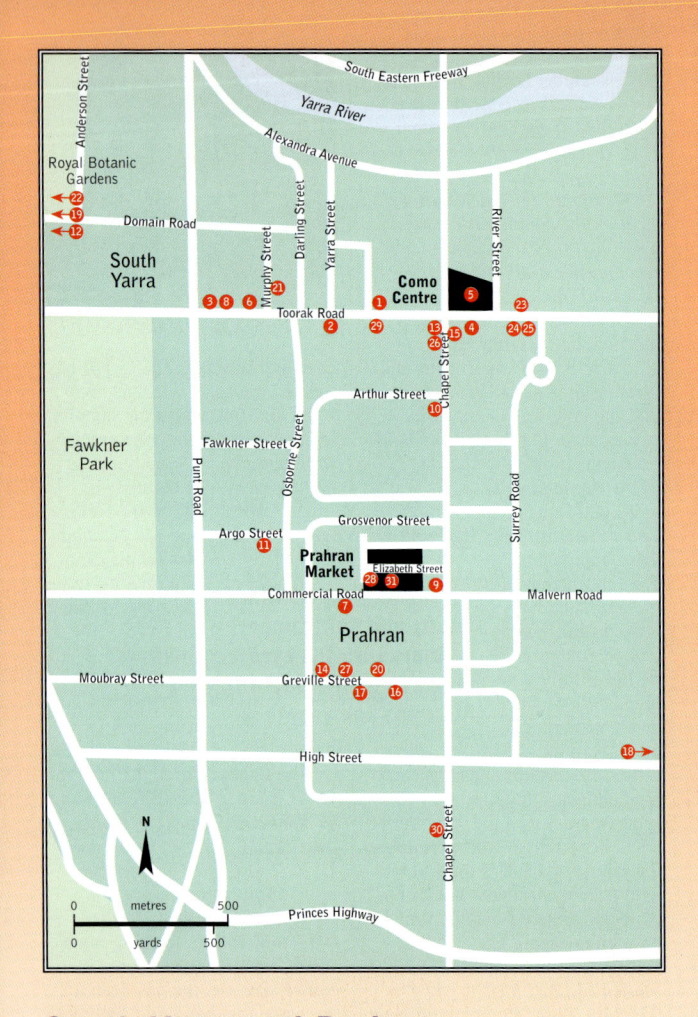

South Yarra and Prahran

South Yarra, and its two main streets of Toorak Rd and trendy Chapel St, represents the height of expensive designer chic in Melbourne's suburbs. Its hip cafés and restaurants overflow with the fashion set, pin-striped merchant bankers, youthful soap opera celebrities, gracious 'ladies who lunch' and just the plain rich.

SOUTH YARRA AND PRAHRAN
Restaurants

Café Grossi ❶

199 Toorak Rd, South Yarra
📞 03-9827 6076
🚋 Tram 8 from Flinders St Station in the city centre into Toorak Rd or train from Flinders St Station to South Yarra Station on the Sandringham/Frankston line

Open: lunch Mon–Fri 1200–1500; dinner Mon–Thu 1800–2230, Fri–Sat 1800–2330

Reservations recommended

All credit cards accepted

Italian

$$

The Grossi family cut their teeth on Café Grossi before taking over the prestigious **Grossi Florentino** restaurant in the city (*see page 16*) and it has been maintained as a top-notch establishment showcasing regional Italian cooking. While the regular menu has many Italian favourites such as *prosciutto* with fresh figs and eggplant *parmigiana*, the daily and seasonal specials hold a greater element of surprise for the more adventurous.

Chinois ❷

176 Toorak Rd, South Yarra
📞 03-9826 3388
🚋 Tram 8 from Flinders St Station in the city centre into Toorak Rd or train from Flinders St Station to South Yarra Station on the Sandringham/Frankston line

Open: lunch Mon–Fri 1200–1500, dinner Mon–Sat from 1800

Reservations essential

All credit cards accepted

Asian fusion

$$$

▲ Chinois

In the early 1990s Chinois led Melbourne dining into the brave new world of Asian fusion food, and is still showing the way in the mixing and matching of Asian and Australian flavours and ingredients. In its bold and dashing main downstairs restaurant, where the rich and famous regularly mingle, the menu will often contain fusions such as Caesar salad with *teriyaki* beef, Chinese roast duck with butternut pumpkin and honey, and coriander-marinated flathead fillets served with *kipfler* potatoes and a *laksa* sauce.

France Soir ❸

11 Toorak Rd, South Yarra
📞 03-9866 8569
🚋 Tram 8 from Flinders St Station in the city centre into Toorak Rd or train from Flinders St Station to South Yarra Station on the Sandringham/Frankston line

Open: daily 1200–1500, 1800–2400

Reservations essential

All credit cards accepted

French

$$

For Francophiles, France Soir is a small piece of heaven; from its waiters in their long, white aprons, to its perfect

South Yarra and Prahran | 39

▲ Cellar at France Soir

baguette bread and the *menu du jour* written on the gilt mirror. Ever popular, and always with high standards, France Soir is a classy yet buzzing place for either dinner or lunch. The menu is classic French bistro, everything from onion soup and *escargots*, to *lapin* (rabbit) sausages, steak *frites*, boeuf bourguignon, steak tartare and even traditional duck *confit*.

Hagger's ❹

268 Toorak Rd, South Yarra
☏ 03-9827 7733
🚊 Tram 8 from Flinders St Station in the city centre into Toorak Rd or train from Flinders St Station to South Yarra Station on the Sandringham/Frankston line
Open: lunch Mon–Fri 1200–1500, dinner daily 1800–2400
Reservations recommended
All credit cards accepted
Modern Australian
$$

Hagger's has escaped from the days when its food was all heavy, its wine hearty and its lunches only ever long and liquid. Now it is a cosy restaurant with a warm yet efficient ambience, offering a bright menu of modern Australian food. Some courses show a blending of, for example, fresh fish with touches of Asian flavours and noodles; while other choices are warm salads, hearty soups and contemporary lamb and beef dishes. Leave room for dessert!

Maxim's ❺

Como Centre, 632 Chapel St (corner of Toorak Rd), South Yarra
☏ 03-9866 5500
🚊 Tram 8 from Flinders St Station in the city centre into Toorak Rd or train from Flinders St Station to South Yarra Station on the Sandringham/Frankston line
Open: Mon–Sat from 1830
Reservations essential
All credit cards accepted
French
$$$

Don't venture into Maxim's inner sanctuary unless you are well-dressed, preferably with pearls and diamonds, well-known, well-heeled and have been part of Melbourne society for at least all of the 40 years that Maxim's has been open. That might be a slight exaggeration, but whereas Maxim's in Paris has an air of high-society frivolity, this restaurant is staid, serious and seriously plush. The food is mainly classical French, complete with rich sauces, lobster *bisque* and the chocolate soufflé signature dish, and a fixed-price menu is also offered.

Da Noi ❻

95 Toorak Rd, South Yarra
☏ 03-9866 5975
🚊 Tram 8 from Flinders St Station in the city centre into Toorak Rd or train from Flinders St Station to South Yarra Station on the Sandringham/Frankston line
Open: lunch Mon–Fri 1200–1500, Sun from 1130; dinner daily from 1800
Reservations recommended
All credit cards accepted
Sardinian
$$

There's not much of a menu here, as owner-chef Pietro Porcu cooks what he feels like each day, depending on what is in season and what makes the best-balanced meal. But be grateful, the result is a well-flavoured, unadorned treat, accompanied by Italian wines. A set-price chef's menu sees Pietro sending out many small and marvellously tasty rustic Sardinian dishes, from *antipasto* complete with suckling pig slices, *linguini neri* topped with saffron, garlic, chilli and yabbies, a *zuppa* Mediterranean fish stew, to roast lamb and eggplant.

Onions [7]

50 Commercial Rd, Prahran

☏ 03-9521 4646

🚊 Tram 8 or 72 from Flinders St Station in the city centre into Toorak Rd or Commercial Rd, or tram 78 or 79 along Chapel St

Open: lunch Tue–Fri 1200–1500, dinner Tue–Sat 1830–late

Reservations recommended

All credit cards accepted

Modern

$$$

This small and slightly out-of-the-way restaurant has grown from being a reliable bistro serving regular locals to one of Melbourne's most accomplished smaller establishments. Both romantic and cosy, Onions' food is harder to categorise, combining a mix of French, modern Australian and new-wave British ideas to create its own eclectic menu. Food is always seasonal, vegetables and potatoes come separately with every main course but at no extra charge, and the choices are guaranteed to be interesting and unique.

pomme [8]

37 Toorak Rd, South Yarra

☏ 03-9820 9606

🚊 Tram 8 from Flinders St Station in the city centre into Toorak Rd or train from Flinders St Station to South Yarra Station on the Sandringham/Frankston line

Open: lunch Sun–Fri 1200–1430, dinner Mon–Sat, 1830–2230

Reservations essential

All credit cards accepted

Modern British

$$$

Just as its near-neighbour France Soir is to Francophiles, pomme is the showcase of new-wave Modern British cooking, under the guidance of part-owner, chef and star modern talent in Melbourne, Jeremy Strode. It also manages to satisfy several sections of its dining audience with brilliant minimalist food, a daily *dégustation* menu and a wide range of vegetarian and game and offal choices. Service is always impeccable, the restaurant modern, chic and airy, and the food exceptional, even if the prices are steeper.

Sweet Basil [9]

209 Commercial Rd, Prahran

☏ 03-9827 3390

🚊 Tram 8 or 72 from Flinders St Station in the city centre into Toorak Rd or Commercial Rd, or tram 78 or 79 along Chapel St

Open: dinner Tue–Sun from 1800

Reservations recommended

All credit cards accepted

Thai

$

Tucked away in a busy café strip near the entrance to the Prahran Market, Sweet Basil is a simple yet slightly trendy modern Thai restaurant, which fits perfectly into its fashionable surroundings. But the food is genuine Thai, from its red curry seafood and stir-fried beef with basil to coconut ice cream and sago pudding.

The Tandoor [10]

517 Chapel St, South Yarra

☏ 03-9827 8247

🚊 Tram 8 from Flinders St Station in the city centre into Toorak Rd, or tram 78 or 79 along Chapel St

Open: lunch Tue–Fri from 1200, dinner Mon–Sat 1800–late

Reservations essential

All credit cards accepted

Indian

$$

The white-starched tablecloths give this Indian favourite a formal look, but inside the atmosphere is relaxed and the food enticing and suitably spicy. For vegetarians there are countless choices, from pumpkin tandoori to the lentil pancake wrapped around a spicy potato curry. But there is also impeccable chicken tandoori cooked in the traditional clay oven and a choice of smaller, *tapas*-style dishes to allow a table to sample as many different tastes as possible.

SOUTH YARRA AND PRAHRAN
Bars, cafés and pubs

The Argo Inn [11]
64 Argo St, South Yarra
✆ 03-9867 3344

The main restaurant of The Argo Hotel is languid and peaceful and serves food typified as modern Australian but is a little more interesting and creative than the standard stuff.

The Botanical Hotel [12]
169 Domain Rd, South Yarra
✆ 03-9866 1684

With its big glass windows, its chrome bars, bright eating space and modern Australian menu of risottos, duck, lamb shanks and so on, this hotel is also regarded as one of Melbourne's best pub restaurants.

Café e Cucina [13]
581 Chapel St, South Yarra
✆ 03-9827 4139

Café e Cucina can be a casual café, an excellent restaurant, an informal bistro or a classy wine bar, depending on what you are looking for and what time of day you pass by. Its Italian credentials are never in doubt, from its great bread and olive oil to its espresso coffee and Italian-accented waiters.

Café Feedwell [14]
95 Greville St, Prahran
✆ 03-9510 3128

For vegetarians, Café Feedwell, in the heart of the bohemian Greville St strip, has been at the forefront of the vegetarian food craze for 30 years and, although only open for dinners on Friday nights, remains a great place to have a cheap and filling vegetarian lunch, breakfast or snack.

Callis and Forrest [15]
572 Chapel St, South Yarra
✆ 03-9827 4854

Lacking the pretensions of some other South Yarra Italian eateries, Callis and Forrest has a good reputation as a quick and good-value Italian bistro, where the *penne* pesto and marsala *zabaglione* dessert are raved about.

Candy Bar [16]
162 Greville St, Prahran
✆ 03-9529 6566

If it's beautiful people and soap opera celebrities you want to mix with, the Candy Bar may be more your scene for an after-work or shopping drink and *tapas* or late-night snacks and cocktails.

The Continental Café [17]
132–4 Greville St, Prahran
✆ 03-9510 2788

The Continental Café is open from 0700 in the morning to late at night and never stops bumping with live music, its own bar, continuous coffee and hearty pasta and pizza meals. This is the place for those who enjoy hanging out with a martini in one hand, cigarette in the other, a strong coffee on the table and live music thumping out from within.

La Couronne [18]
412 High St, Prahran
✆ 03-9510 3751

For lovers of French breakfasts, with their baguettes, big bowls of coffee and hot chocolate, pains au chocolat and croissants, La Couronne is a simple French café and patisserie tucked away from the Chapel St hubbub. It also serves lovely light French lunches of quiches, filled baguettes, pastries, tarts and salads.

Garden Kiosk [19]
Royal Botanic Gardens main entrance, Birdwood Ave., South Yarra

Inside the formal gardens by the main Ornamental Lake is the Garden Kiosk, which has been transformed into an elegant licensed café, ideal for afternoon tea, a glass of wine or a gentle place to sit in the sun amidst the peace of the gardens.

Greville Bar 20

143 Greville St, Prahran
✆ 03-9529 4800

The Greville Bar with its tiny timber interior, soft jazz tunes and candles on the table is the place for an intimate romantic evening or midnight rendezvous (it's open until 0300 from Thu to Sat) away from the bright lights and people-watchers.

Harveys 21

10 Murphy St, South Yarra
✆ 03-9867 3605

Open from 0700, Harveys, in the heart of Toorak Rd territory, has tables out on the terrace in summer and by the fireplace for winter, and is the epicentre of breakfast money-making, with its great porridge, fruit mueslis, fresh orange juice, omelettes and eggs 'n' bacon.

Observatory Café 22

Royal Botanic Gardens main entrance, Birdwood Ave., South Yarra
✆ 03-9650 5600

This newcomer is set in a new modern visitors' centre complex amongst the peaceful white domes and telescopes of the former Observatory in magnificent formal English gardens laid out with lakes, ducks, lawns, fern gullies and sweeping vistas. It's excellent for eggs, muesli, coffee and brunch, or even buying meat and cooking it on the barbecue provided.

Sushi Belt 23

313 Toorak Rd, South Yarra
✆ 03-9827 4199

A casual sushi counter café where prepared sushi and *sashimi* dishes glide past diners on a revolving conveyor belt holding colour-coded set-price trays and dishes.

Viet's Quan 24

Shop 6, 300 Toorak Rd, South Yarra
✆ 03-9827 4765

Even among the height of hipness in South Yarra, real Vietnamese food can be found at Viet's Quan, where fashionable furniture and orange walls don't detract from the authentic and reasonably priced food being served, with all its tangy and delicious flavours of rice-paper spring rolls, Vietnamese mint and fish with lime dressing.

▲ Observatory Café

SOUTH YARRA AND PRAHRAN
Shops, markets and picnic sites

Shops

Edokko Mart 25
322 Toorak Rd, South Yarra
☎ 03-9827 4519

For Japanese devotees, Edokko Mart stocks all the basic necessities of Japanese cuisine, from special rice and seaweed to tofu and pickled vegetables, as well as Kirin beer and *sake*.

Greek Deli and Taverna 26
583 Chapel St, South Yarra
☎ 03-9827 3734

For lovers of Greek food, this noisy and fun deli sells takeaway dips and Greek meals, as well as being a boisterous place to eat casually and well.

Greens and Grains 27
123 Greville St, Prahran
☎ 03-9510 4256

For organic food, the place to go is Greens and Grains, which stocks everything from biodynamic fruit and vegetables, macrobiotic products including Japanese ingredients, free-range eggs, and organic grains and breads.

Hotsville 17
1/126 Greville St, Prahran
☎ 03-9510 5666

This place is heaven for chilli addicts with its imported chilli sauces, chilli cookbooks and even chilli ice cream and chocolate.

let's eat 28
Elizabeth St, Prahran
☎ 03-9520 3287

let's eat is an experiment in a new integrated approach to up-market food by giant Australian retailer Coles Myer. It is set in a magnificent, cavernous and up-beat shop, which is beautifully designed and decorated. The store combines fresh produce such as meats, chicken and seafood stalls, with top-of-the-range cooking utensil displays, a wine bar and wine store, a food section selling prepared meals ready to take home and cook, and a bistro kitchen serving meals in a casual upstairs restaurant. Nothing is cheap, but the pilot idea (it may be extended to other parts of Australia) clearly appeals to the many affluent singles and couples who live in Prahran and South Yarra who are cash-rich but time-poor.

Marrons Glacés 29
192 Toorak Rd, South Yarra
☎ 03-9827 7197

Ice-cream fanatics are best advised to pop in here to try *gelati* flavours such as *baci*, *zabaglione*, lemon, pistachio and coffee.

Paterson's Cakes 30
117 Chapel St, Windsor
☎ 03-9510 8541

The kingdom of cakes in Melbourne is Paterson's Cakes, which for 84 years has been making and selling its magnificent-tasting and decorated cakes to the birthday parties of the rich and famous. Some of its favourite delicacies on offer include apple Charlottes, chocolate rum truffles, rainbow sponges and Mississippi mud cake.

Markets

Prahran Market 31
163-85 Commercial Rd, Prahran
☎ 03-9522 3302
Open: Tue, Thu, Fri and Sat dawn–1700

Locals who talk about this food and produce market with hushed tones clearly regard their shopping expeditions here as akin to a visit to a food temple mixed with a weekly social occasion. Friends arrange to meet at the market for coffee, or impromptu dinner party invitations are extended over the oyster, fish and crayfish displays.

Speciality stalls at the Prahran Market well worth a visit include **Curry Creations** (*shop 42-4*) with its excellent range of Indian curry pastes and spices; **Damian Pike's Wild Mushrooms** stall (*stand 429-31*) which stocks fresh and dried mushrooms of every exotic variety imaginable (and more), including fresh truffles when in season; **Farm Fresh Eggs** (*stall 49-50*) with its honey and fresh eggs (everything from free-range and quail eggs, to emu and ostrich eggs); and **Hagen's Herbs and Gourmet Salads** (*stall 419-23*) with all the fresh herbs, such as tarragon, hot mint, curry leaves, lemongrass, kaffir lime leaves and Vietnamese mint, that are often hard to find, as well as the more common herbs, and a cornucopia of lettuce varieties and salad leaves. The freshest fish and seafood is at **Bracher Seafood** (*shop 512*), as well as a resident sushi chef; **Cester's Poultry and Game** (*shop 506*) stocks all your poultry and game requirements from turkeys, chickens, quails, ducks and spatchcock to rabbits and kangaroo, while opposite, at Shop 509, the same John Cester's **Select Foods** sells a range of ready-to-cook fresh pastas, pies, *parmigianas*, sausages and gourmet chipolatas. The best delicatessen is probably **Cleo's Deli**, which makes many of its own products such as pasta, *gnocchi*, dips and marinated *antipasto*, and also sells one of Melbourne's best selection of breads and local cheeses.

▲ Prahran Market

Dining on the move

The royal treatment

One of Melbourne's major tourist attractions – especially one with a gourmet touch – is the world's only restaurant situated in a moving tram. Dining in **The Colonial Tramcar Restaurant** (*departs: tram stop No 125, Normanby Rd, South Melbourne; ∅ 03-9696 4000; tram along Spencer St or Clarendon St to Crown Casino; open: two daily dinner sittings, either 1745–1915 or 2035–2330, also Sun lunch tour; reservations essential; all credit cards accepted; Modern Australian;* ❸❸❸) is a unique highlight of many visitors' stay in Melbourne. It is a restaurant that disproves the gourmand's adage never to eat in any restaurant that moves, revolves or floats. The Colonial Tramcar serves a five-course set-price dinner of remarkably high standard.

Australian sparkling wine from the Yarra Valley is sipped and pâté nibbled as the easily recognisable tram, glowing outside with lights, crosses the Yarra River, and rattles past the Victorian landmark of Flinders St Station and the spire of the Victorian Arts Centre. A starter of either pepper-encrusted kangaroo fillets or slices of smoked Tasmanian salmon is served, accompanied by a local Shiraz and Chardonnay, as the Colonial Tramcar glides along St Kilda Rd and enters the streets of the affluent leafy suburbs of South Yarra and Toorak.

Not only is the meal memorable for its Australian wines and cuisine, but the setting in the plush 1927 burgundy and gold tramcar is opulent; you are greeted by velvet and teak fittings and brass lamps reminiscent of the elegant roaring 1920s.

The tram, which is always filled with a mixture of celebrating locals and visiting overseas tourists, next takes a tour down the tram tracks of Melbourne's popular Toorak Rd and Chapel St precinct. A main course of fresh eye fillet steak or French chicken is then served.

The cosy intimate dining experience continues with dessert

▲ The Colonial Tramcar Restaurant

as the Colonial Tramcar explores the spacious suburbs of Toorak, Malvern, Balaclava and Caulfield. Finally, the palm trees that line the Port Phillip Bay are reached and, as the yachts on the water glisten silver in the moonlight, coffee, chocolates and liqueurs are brought round. The bright lights of St Kilda – which never sleeps – come and go, until the Colonial Tramcar finally finishes its dinner tour back where it started by the Yarra River. As most patrons stagger home replete after their five-course dinner, others decide to continue to party on at the casino or in the surrounding bars and cafés that line Southbank.

Another of Melbourne's transport icons is the historic **Puffing Billy** steam train (*departs: Belgrave Station, the Dandenong Hills; ✆ 03-9754 6800; ◉ take a normal suburban train (Belgrave Line) from Flinders St Station in the city centre or a one-hour drive from the city centre via Burwood Hwy; open: lunch train departs Mon–Fri 1200, except public and school holidays, night train departs all year Fri–Sat 1900; reservations recommended for lunch train but essential for night train; all credit cards accepted; light lunch, old-style Australian dinners;* ❺❺–❺❺❺) that chugs amidst the ferns and towering gum trees of the Dandenongs, having opened its brass doors as a regular restaurant train.

> ... disproves the gourmand's adage never to eat in any restaurant that moves, revolves or floats ...

As Puffing Billy slowly steams along under sunny mountain skies, guests are offered hot soup, then a choice of a simple cheese and fruit hamper or quiche lunch, or a magnificent gourmet hamper containing smoked trout, complementary chutneys and pink roast beef as well. Wines and beer can be bought on the train as it continues along its journey, stopping at the **Steam Museum** at Menzies Creek, and then at **Emerald Lake Park**, before returning to Belgrave by 1530. On Friday and Saturday nights, Puffing Billy turns into an enchanted world, offering visitors to Melbourne a dinner-dance experience with a real bush flavour. The night train leaves Belgrave Station at 1900, pottering along the 11km track through the bush while free pre-dinner nibbles are served, before stopping at the rustic Packing Shed along the line near Emerald. Here guests disembark from the train for a three-course meal of soup, a hot carvery with roast lamb, scotch fillet, turkey, and dessert smorgasbord, including wines. A log fire blazes while an entertainer plays music and old-time dancing quickly takes over the magical night. At about 2245, the polished brass and blue steam train is re-boarded for the final chug through the dark forests of the Dandenong Hills while tea and coffee is served, accompanied by cheese platters, chocolates and port, arriving back at Belgrave at 2345.

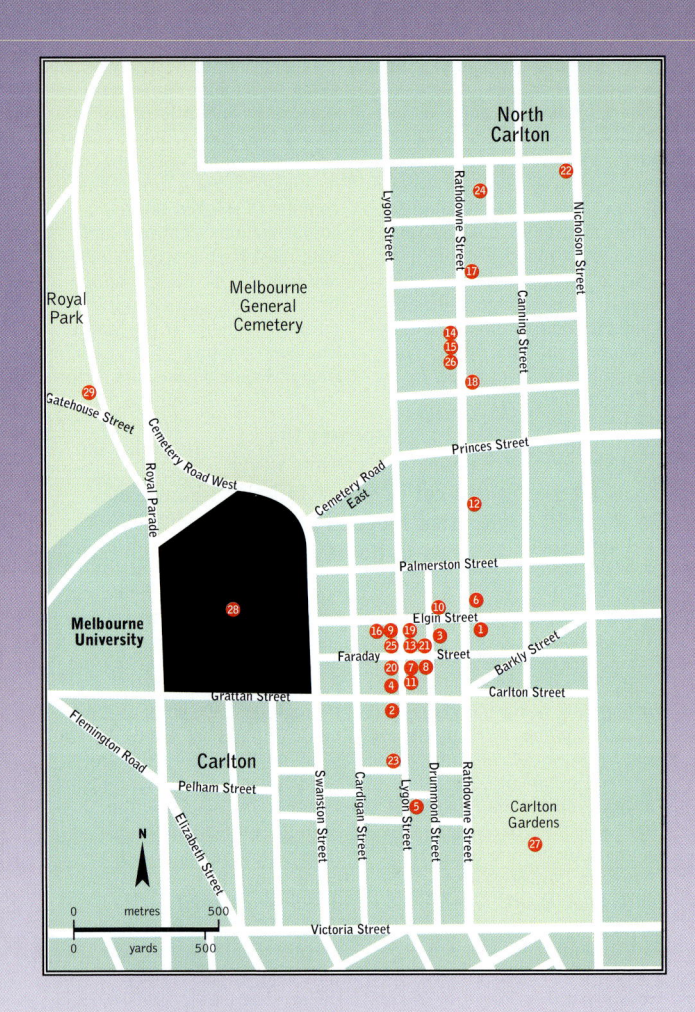

Carlton and Lygon St

The Carlton area fringes the northern edge of Melbourne's city centre, and since the early 1950s has been a centre of fine food, restaurants and cosmopolitan living, at a time when it was hard to find a decent espresso or buy fresh pasta anywhere else in town.

CARLTON AND LYGON ST
Restaurants

Abla's ❶

109 Elgin St, Carlton
✆ 03-9347 0006
🚆 Tram along Swanston St from the city centre to Melbourne University and Lygon St, or bus 200 or 201 from Russell St, City, along Lygon St and Elgin St
Open: lunch Thu–Fri 1200–1500, dinner Mon–Sat 1800–2300
Reservations recommended
All credit cards accepted
Lebanese
$$

For anyone who thought Lebanese food was simple and monotonous, Abla's intimate restaurant run by matriarch Abla Amad proves time and time again that Middle Eastern food can be artistic, homely and authentic. There are tasty dips, delicate pastries, seasoned grills and wonderful eggplant, fish and kofta specials. The best option is the generous banquet so you can sample a little of all that is great about Lebanese cooking; indeed it is mandatory on busy Friday and Saturday nights for tables of more than two people.

Le Café Francais ❷

163 Grattan St, Carlton
✆ 03-9349 1888
🚆 Tram along Swanston St from the city centre to Melbourne University, Grattan St stop, or bus 200 or 201 from Russell St, City, along Lygon St
Open: Tue–Sat 1900–late
Reservations essential
All credit cards accepted
French
$$$

Le Café Francais has the atmosphere of a country *auberge* run by a provincial French family. Open only for dinner, and strictly BYO (bring your own alcohol), this little restaurant focuses on cooking perfectly just a few dishes from a small menu, as well as always having blackboard specials depending on seasonal fresh produce. There are old favourites such as rabbit in mustard *jus*, fillet of beef with a pepper sauce, and duck with Grand Marnier.

Donnini's ❸

312 Drummond St, Carlton
✆ 03-9347 3128
🚆 Tram along Swanston St from the city centre to Melbourne University and Lygon St, or bus 200 or 201 from Russell St, City, along Lygon St and Elgin St
Open: daily 1200–1500, 1800–late
Reservations recommended
All credit cards accepted
Italian
$

Donnini's is a Melbourne restaurant classic, run by the famous Donnini pasta family and popular for decades with the local literary and intellectual set. Its dining room is always crowded and its Italian food is simple, ample and inexpensive – if you're really hungry try the *antipasto* plate followed by its signature three-pasta platter.

Il Gambero ❹

215 Lygon St, Carlton
✆ 03-9347 5791
🚆 Tram along Swanston St from the city centre to Melbourne University, Grattan St stop, or bus 200 or 201 from Russell St, City, along Lygon St
Open: Mon–Fri 1130–1500, 1700–late; Sat 1130–0100; Sun 1100–2300
Reservations unnecessary
All credit cards accepted
Italian
$

This rowdy Italian restaurant is a popular haunt of university students, both past and present. Its name means 'the prawn' in Italian, and its garlic prawns are both exceptional

Carlton and Lygon St | 49

▲ Tiamo is one of Lygon Street's oldest Italian bistros

and justifiably famous (don't forget a toothbrush if you want your dinner guests to talk to you later!). Eating here is about dining cheaply and in warm and noisy surroundings – with the pizza-tossing by the chefs behind the open kitchen bar a great feature.

Lemongrass ❺

176 Lygon St, Carlton

✆ 03-9662 2244

🚊 Tram along Swanston St from the city centre to Melbourne University, stop at Queensberry St or Grattan St, or bus 200 or 201 from Russell St, City, along Lygon St

Open: lunch Mon–Sat 1200–1430, dinner daily 1730–2230

Reservations recommended

Thai

❸❸

This is one of Melbourne's finest Thai restaurants serving what it calls Royal Thai cuisine. Based on ancient Siam recipes, there are the standard excellent green and red curries, but also a mass of enticing and more unusual dishes such as *poo ja* – stuffed blue swimmer crab – and the green papaya salad. The décor is modern, but with some elegant touches of bamboo and silk without verging on the kitsch.

Paris-Go Bistro ❻

116 Rathdowne St, Carlton

✆ 03-9347 7507

🚊 Tram along Swanston St from the city centre to Melbourne University and Lygon St, or bus 200 or 201 from Russell St, City, along Lygon St and Elgin St

Open: Tue–Sun 1800–late

Reservations recommended

All credit cards accepted

French

❸❸

This traditional French bistro, complete with white paper tablecloths and French-accented waiters, serves classic French-style meals in bubbly, informal surroundings. The food is rich, creamy, wine-based and reliable; at Paris-Go it sometimes seems that the *frites* are always crisp, the chicken liver pâté smooth and the crème brûlée always light.

Shakahari ❼

201–3 Faraday St, Carlton

✆ 03-9347 3848

🚊 Tram along Swanston St from the city centre to Melbourne University, Faraday St stop, or bus 200 or 201 from Russell St, City, along Lygon St

Open: lunch Mon–Sat 1200–1530, dinner Sun–Thu 1800–2130, Fri–Sat 1800–2230

Reservations recommended

All credit cards accepted

Vegetarian

❸❸

You can eat here on either a tight budget or

splash out a little more – either way, all the dishes demonstrate how vegetarian fare need not always be dull, monotonous or based around lentils and mungbeans. Most dishes are vegan and many have Asian influences, such as the warm tofu with Thai dressing, Malaysian curry bliss or the Asiatic lasagne.

Sicilian Vespers ❽

295 Drummond St, corner of Faraday St, Carlton

✆ 03-9347 0199

🚋 Tram along Swanston St from the city centre to Melbourne University, Faraday St stop, or bus 200 or 201 from Russell St, City, along Lygon St

Open: Tue–Sun 1200–1500, 1800–late

Reservations recommended

All credit cards accepted

Italian

$$

Named after the famous 13th-century rebellion when the Sicilian people rose up against French invaders – and later immortalised in a Verdi opera – Sicilian Vespers serves contemporary Italian regional food in quiet surroundings. Some of the dishes such as the risottos and meats are based on rustic Sicilian flavours, but other regional specialities such as truffles from Umbria and Tuscany are also featured.

Tiamo ❾

303–5 Lygon St, Carlton

✆ 03-9347 5759

🚋 Tram along Swanston St from the city centre to Melbourne University or bus 200 or 201 from Russell St, City, along Lygon St

Open: Mon–Sat 0730–2330, Sun 0930–2230

Reservations unnecessary

💳 VISA

Italian

$

If you are in search of a simple, old-style Italian restaurant and you don't mind being surrounded by the bustle of generations of university students, writers, Italian families and clinking wine bottles, the original Tiamo restaurant and espresso bar is for you. It serves good wholesome Italian fare, all cheaply priced and served speedily in cramped, dark and garlic-filled surroundings. But Tiamo means 'I love you' in Italian and most of those people in-the-know love this busy restaurant too.

Toofey's ❿

162 Elgin St, corner Drummond St, Carlton

✆ 03-9347 9838

🚋 Tram along Swanston St from city centre to Melbourne University and Lygon St, or bus 200 or 201 from Russell St, City, along Lygon St and Elgin St

Open: Tue–Fri 1200–1430, 1800–2230; Sat–Sun 1800–2230

Reservations essential

All credit cards accepted

Seafood

$$

If Toofey's had deliberately set out to prove there was more to dining in Carlton than pasta and pizza, it couldn't have made its point more effectively. Regularly winning awards as Melbourne's best seafood restaurant, this elegant eating house set in an old two-storey corner shop serves magnificently fresh fish, shellfish and crustaceans. The simple cooking style never dominates the raw ingredients, but the sauces and oriental touches take the seafood to another culinary plane.

▲ Toofey's roast local snapper

CARLTON AND LYGON ST
Bars, cafés and pubs

292 Wine Bar [11]

292 Lygon St, Carlton
℡ 03-9349 1299

If *Jimmy Watson's* (*see page 53*) is old-style Carlton, 292 Wine Bar is all new Carlton, with its paved floor, timber bar and brown leather walls decorating a narrow, deep restaurant space. Drop in for a quick bite or turn up on Sunday afternoons for the jazz sessions.

Arc Café [12]

160 Rathdowne St, Carlton
℡ 03-9349 3933

Once just a small café, the Arc Café is now regarded as one of Melbourne's best BYO bistros, with wine connoisseurs flocking to its lunch and dinner tables with their best bottles to accompany the innovative food served up by this modest, shopfront café.

Brunetti Caffé [13]

198 Faraday St, Carlton
℡ 03-9347 6191

Saturday morning shopping in Carlton, or indeed at any time of the day, night or week, wouldn't be complete without a coffee and sweet cake or nibble from Brunetti. With its fake and glitzy decorations, this popular café-restaurant, which has sprawled into three adjoining shops and outside on to the pavement, brings a touch of stylish Rome to bustling Carlton, whether you are drinking coffee, eating its cakes, licking its *gelati* or dining in its side restaurant, which specialises in Rome's favourite *saltimbocca* and *ossobuco*.

The Carlton Paragon Café [14]

651 Rathdowne St, North Carlton
℡ 03-9349 7715

▲ Lygon St cafés

A popular and old-time favourite is the light, airy and good-value Paragon Café located in a grand old Victorian building. It serves everything from breakfast to dinners and soups, coffees and risottos, all with a relaxed cheerful ambience.

La Casa del Caffè ⑮

649 Rathdowne St, North Carlton
✆ 03-9347 1851

For cakes, coffee and handmade chocolates, it's hard to go past La Casa del Caffè. A family-run coffee shop, most of the regulars are known by name, and although it serves lunches and light meals with soups and *focaccias*, it's the cakes and coffee that keep the locals coming back.

Jimmy Watson's Wine Bar ⑯

333 Lygon St, Carlton
✆ 03-9347 3985

A grand tradition among wine buffs was started 60 years ago, when Jimmy Watson's Wine Bar opened, offering a place to taste wines and share opened bottles in an atmosphere of intellectual camaraderie. Beloved of university lecturers and the Carlton set, this is the place to just sit and enjoy a glass of wine or a casual lunch (especially popular before the Saturday afternoon football) or dinner of modern European fare.

The Kent Hotel ⑰

370 Rathdowne St, North Carlton
✆ 03-9347 5672

This hotel used to be a workers' pub, but as the streets became more leafy and young professionals moved into North Carlton, The Kent moved with the times and now serves three meals a day – and anything in-between you fancy – of its modern Australian fare. There's an informal bar, plus a bistro, and outdoor tables overlooking the park next door.

La Luna Bistro ⑱

320 Rathdowne St, North Carlton
✆ 03-9349 4888

La Luna Bistro is a great favourite with locals for dinner and lunch, but it is its up-market brunches on the weekend which should not be missed.

trotters

Trotters ⑲

400 Lygon St, Carlton
✆ 03-9347 5657

Breakfast at Trotters is a Lygon St institution, serving great eggs Benedict, bacon and fresh orange juice. Sit outside on the footpath over breakfast, reading the papers or watching the world pass by, or drop in anytime for homely lunches and dinners.

Universita Bar and Ristorante ⑳

257 Lygon St, Carlton
✆ 03-9347 0705

Reputedly the second home of Australia's leading trade unionists and political activists, the Universita is all things to all people. Downstairs it is a café and casual bar where students and Lygon St shoppers congregate, while upstairs is the home of the heavier political debates over hearty plates of Italian food.

Carlton and Lygon St | 53

CARLTON AND LYGON ST
Shops, markets and picnic sites

Shops

Brunetti's [21]

200 Faraday St, Carlton
☏ 03-9347 2801

One of Melbourne's great Italian cake shops, Brunetti's is a place that sweet-tooths and Italian aficionados can't afford to miss. Attached to the popular coffee shop, Brunetti's makes and sells all the old Italian favourites – *cannoncini* (chocolate and vanilla custard tarts), *diplomatici* (puff pastry and liqueur custards) and the full range of *ricciarelle* (ground almond), hazelnut and amaretti biscuits.

Canals [22]

703 Nicholson St, North Carlton
☏ 03-9380 4537

The best seafood in Melbourne has long been said to be available from Canals family seafood shop which has been selling some of the freshest and best-quality seafood in the city since 1931. The array of seafood is a delight to behold – scallops in their shells, the full range of pacific and native oysters from Tasmania, Victoria and South Australia, yabbies from the rivers, King George whiting, pink Atlantic salmon and succulent crayfish in summer.

Casa del Gelato [23]

161 Lygon St, Carlton
☏ 03-9347 0220

Don't forget to drop into Casa del Gelato for the most delectable homemade *gelati* you are ever likely to taste in your life. All *gelati* are made on the premises, and the lemon, chocolate, *zabaglione* and coffee flavours are to die for.

Donati's Fine Meats [19]

402 Lygon St, Carlton
☏ 03-9347 4948

This butcher is Italian through and through, his shanks are sliced ready for *ossobuco*, the true veal is *scaloppine*-perfect, and dangling in the front window is always a huge *cotechnico* sausage (a gelatinous pork salami). Offal is big here, with hearts, ox tongues, oxtails, tripe and calves' liver all ready for your favourite Italian sweetbread dish.

Donnini's Pasta [19]

398 Lygon St, Carlton
☏ 03-9347 1655

This family business, which was the first store in Melbourne to produce and sell fresh pasta once Italian immigrants started coming to Melbourne, starts making fresh pasta at 0200 each morning at the back of the shop. Its window is always filled with a tempting and colourful array of *linguine*, *pappardelle*, *tagliatelle* and *rigatoni*, with some elegant filled pastas also made, such as the salmon and ricotta *agnolotti*, or the chicken and veal *tortellini*. Ready-made sauces are also sold.

Enoteca Sileno [24]

21 Amess St, North Carlton
☏ 03-9347 5044

The mecca of all Italian food stores is North Carlton's Enoteca Sileno where anyone dreaming of the best Italian squid ink, the best risotto, the most beautiful handmade pastas and the most perfect display of boutique Italian olive oils will not be disappointed.

Grinders Coffee House [20]

277 Lygon St, Carlton
☏ 03-9347 7520

Sometimes known as Torrefazione Caffè, this

54 | Carlton and Lygon St

place has been setting the standards for selling coffee on Lygon St since 1962. It is the quintessential Italian coffee house, pokey and cramped, but with the beans roasted out the back, its shop filled with every type of coffee and coffee-making equipment imaginable, and a magnificent smell of fresh coffee wafting out of its front door.

King And Godfree 25

293–7 Lygon St, Carlton
✆ 03-9347 1619

Almost any fresh picnic ingredient can be bought at King And Godfree but, most importantly, it is also the best wine stockist in Lygon St, with an excellent range of Australian and Italian wines at good-value prices, especially some of the cleanskin specials.

Melbourne Cheese House 20

Lygon Food Store, 263 Lygon St, Carlton
✆ 03-9347 6279

It is impossible to walk past the Melbourne Cheese House without admiring the huge wheels of imported Italian, Swiss and French cheeses that fill its windows, where they are turned and oiled until at least three years of age. There are 120kg rings of Emmental, real *parmigiano reggiano* and true parmesan, as well as a huge range of other soft and hard rind cheeses.

Rathdowne Street Food Store 26

617 Rathdowne St, North Carlton
✆ 03-9347 4064

Where breads, soups, tarts, pastries, pickles and vegetarian lasagne are all cooked by chef Ricky Holt ready to take away to your home kitchen or picnic.

Thresherman's Bakehouse 20

221 Faraday St, Carlton
✆ 03-9349 2319

This is no small, local bakery, but a warehouse-style bakery that has transformed itself into a favourite breakfast and lunch spot, complete with hot dishes, soups, pizzas and a university canteen atmosphere. It also sells a full range of sourdough, *focaccia*, baguettes, naan and Lebanese breads, plus everything from Danish pastries and lamingtons to croissants and pain au chocolat.

Picnic sites

Carlton Gardens 27

Corner of Rathdowne St and Grattan St, Carlton

Adjourn to the local shady Carlton Gardens adjoining Melbourne's new museum and Royal Exhibition Building for a quiet relaxing picnic under the old English trees.

Melbourne University 28

Swanston St, Carlton

An option is to wander around Melbourne University and its many courtyards and cloisters to find a quiet, green spot, although on weekdays this may be hard to come by.

Royal Park 29

Access from corner of Royal Parade and Gatehouse St

Across Carlton in neighbouring Parkville is the extensive Royal Park which is home to many sporting ovals, but also contains a quiet **Australian Native Garden** and the **Melbourne Zoo**.

▲ Donnini's Pasta

The Queen Victoria Market

Victoria's most popular attraction

Even if exploring local markets is one of your favourite travel pastimes, you won't have experienced anything like the **Queen Victoria Market** (*corner of Elizabeth St and Victoria St; ✆ 03-9320 5822; ⓠ trams along Elizabeth St, Queen St or Victoria St, car parking available, underground loop train to Flagstaff or Melbourne Central stations; open: Tue and Thu 0600-1400, Fri 0600-1800, Sat 0600-1500, Sun 0900-1600*) close to Melbourne's heart. A Melbourne institution and a food market unparalleled anywhere in Australia, the 'Queen Vic Market', as it is universally known, is one of Melbourne's must-see experiences.

Open since 1868, the Queen Vic Market sprawls across a seven-hectare site on the city centre's fringe, selling the most wonderful array of fruit, vegetables, meat, seafood and delicatessen items imaginable. This is the place for Britons and Europeans to stare in amazement, as top-quality fillet steak sells for a snip, live crayfish and prawns practically crawl off the fish stall shelves, and as exotic fresh fruit and vegetables from all over Australia and Asia sit in colourful splendour ready to confound even the most knowledgeable fruit lover.

Try and be there before 0900 – although all morning on Saturdays is the most busy and exciting time – for the best of market experiences. The air is filled with the cries of Italian cheese and salami merchants, Aussie butchers, Greek fishmongers, Chinese fruitsellers and Vietnamese flowergrowers. The gourmets' paradise has its home in the dairy produce **Lower Hall**, where the 38 delis offer everything from pâté to caviar, free-range chickens to rabbit and kangaroos, olives to oregano and other spices, and a huge range of local and imported cheeses.

But the Queen Vic Market is also about much more than food. On Saturdays and Sundays its aisles extend out into its sunny car parks and all of its stalls, even in the most outlying corners, are crammed with great value goods. This is the place to buy bargain jeans and jumpers, or leather jackets and ski clothes, party dresses and baby gear.

▲ Queen Victoria Market delicatessen

There are pot plant stalls next to souvenir shops, kitchen utensil outlets next to cheap shoe stalls and jewellery stands intermingled with rolls of the most colourful fabrics from all around the world.

Even if shopping for food is not your forte, the Queen Vic Market – which is free and is rated as Victoria's most popular tourist attraction – is a fantastic place just to people-watch. Many of its legendary stallholders are larger-than-life characters who are performers as much as market merchants. And then there are the real performers: the **buskers** who sing, juggle, fire-eat and play-act their talents around the market.

In recent years, the Queen Vic Market has successfully expanded the number of food outlets selling meals and takeaway nibbles to hungry breakfast patrons and famished shoppers. In summer, from November until January between 1800 and 2200, a new Wednesday **Gaslight Night Market** has been started for those looking for something a bit different. This is the place to come to find high-quality arts and crafts from around the world, to have your fortune read by tarot cards or crystal ball, and to buy all the latest New Age crystals, oils, mirrors and clothes. There are always local bands to listen to amongst the international food stalls. Early in April the **Asian Hawkers Market** is held on three consecutive nights under the Upper Market's sweeping aisles. More than 30 of Melbourne's leading Asian restaurants sell their favourite dishes and courses, in exchange for festival coupons, alongside winery outlets, Indian dancing bands, Japanese noodle-makers and winding Chinese lion dragons.

> **The air is filled with the cries of Italian cheese merchants, Aussie butchers, Greek fishmongers and Chinese fruitsellers.**

The Queen Victoria Market also offers two tours each day the market is open, except on Sundays. The **Heritage Tour** starts at 1030 and visitors will be let into the market's secret history as Melbourne's first cemetery, hear stories of its most colourful, and often reprobate, characters, and learn about its place in Melbourne's rich cultural and architectural heritage. For those more interested in food, the **Foodies Dream Tour**, with its generous sampling of food from around the globe, tantalises the tastebuds and extends the waistline. Starting at 1000, this tour provides tips on market food shopping and selection and gives an insight into the market's huge array of produce and food. Bookings are required.

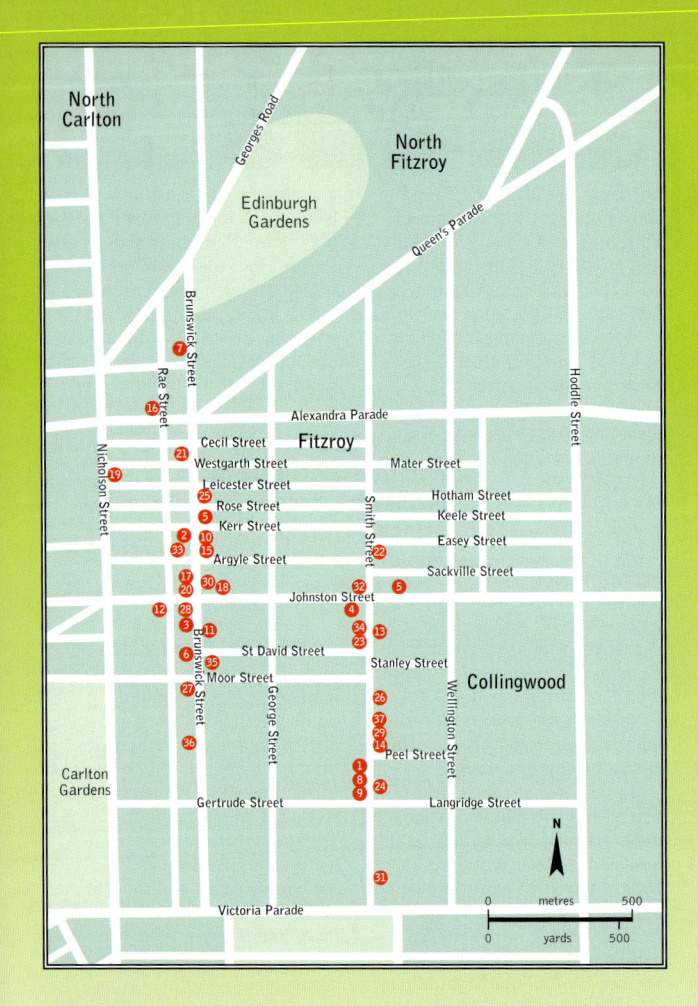

Fitzroy: Brunswick St and Smith St

This once working-class part of inner Melbourne has become a hip centre for the creative café and food scene, without succumbing to superficiality or glitz. Brunswick St is alive with casual cafés, restaurants, food stores, buskers, street performers and pubs, while Smith St has become a second food mecca for alternative lifestylers.

FITZROY: BRUNSWICK ST AND SMITH ST
Restaurants

Café Coco ❶

129 Smith St, Fitzroy
☎ 03-9417 3937
🚊 No 86 tram along Smith St from Victoria Parade and the city centre
Open: Mon-Thu 1100-late, Fri-Sun 0900-late
Reservations recommended
💳 VISA
Modern Australian
$$

Coco has a reputation for understated quality and quiet – an eating haven free of the ideology and political statements that prevail in many neighbouring establishments. Dine cosily in winter in the bottom of a solid two-storey terrace house, or, in summer, eat outdoors under the vines of the leafy courtyard. Perfect for a coffee, light lunch or romantic dinner of excellent noodles, *gnocchi* or risotto.

The Fitz Café ❷

347 Brunswick St, Fitzroy
☎ 03-9417 5794
🚊 Light rail or tram from city up Collins St and along Brunswick St
Open: daily 0700-late
Reservations recommended
💳 VISA
Modern Australian
$

Set on a strategic corner in the heart of Brunswick St's busiest strip, the Fitz is a great place for people-watching, whether over breakfast, lunch or dinner. The food here is eclectic, from the special Fitz salad for two, to Middle-Eastern eggplant baked with chickpeas or free-range chicken.

Guernica ❸

257 Brunswick St, Fitzroy
☎ 03-9416 0969
🚊 Light rail or tram from city up Collins St and along Brunswick St
Open: lunch Mon-Fri 1200-1500, Sun 1200-1600; dinner daily 1800-2230
Reservations essential
All credit cards accepted
Modern Australian
$$

Guernica has been winning culinary praise for years, long before the street became as trendy as it is today. It serves modern Australian food, all with a subtle Asian twist, but that description hardly portrays the long lunches of fine food, wine and conversation for which Guernica is so well known. The coconut-battered and fried garfish is a house signature dish.

Guru Da Dhaba ❹

240 Johnston St, Fitzroy
☎ 03-9486 9155
🚊 Tram along Smith St, Johnston St stop, or Bulleen-bound bus down Elgin St and Johnston St
Open: Mon-Fri 1730-2300, Sat 1230-2330, Sun 1230-1600
Reservations recommended
No credit cards accepted
Indian
$

In the best traditions of *dhabas* (casual Indian eating houses), Guru Da Dhaba serves authentic Indian street food using freshly ground spices. The cheap tasty food, much of it with a northern Indian bent, is some of the best in Melbourne – try the clay tandoori-baked chicken tikka or the creamy Punjabi *gosht sadabahar* (spiced lamb) as well as the excellent mixed vegetable dishes (*subji*). Lunch is only served on weekends, in an Indian 'Chaat' manner: a mix of savoury snacks served *yum-cha* style for the whole table.

Fitzroy: Brunswick St and Smith St | 59

GUERNICA

"...witness Melbourne's most unassuming exponent of finest Aussie cuisine."

STEPHEN DOWNES THE WEEKEND AUSTRALIAN JAN. '99

"...excellent modern Australian food."

WALLPAPER JAN. '99

"...simple dishes of tantalising visual appeal, that also tease the taste buds with bold combinations."

THE AGE GOOD FOOD GUIDE '99

"...chic but not stuffy and the food is divine and the service attentive." Voted best restaurant in its category.

MIETTA'S EATING & DRINKING

Joe's Garage ⑤

366 Brunswick St, Fitzroy

☏ 03-9419 9944

🚊 Light rail or tram from city up Collins St and along Brunswick St

Open: daily 0730–0100

Reservations not allowed

American Express

Modern Australian

$

Very popular with the young, hip and designer-trendy, the food at Joe's Garage is casual and quick, which is fortunate since the crowds can be huge and bookings are not accepted. But the friendly buzzing atmosphere, Joe's famous burgers, the many vegetarian choices and the magnificent cakes keep the crowds flocking back for more.

Kazen ⑥

201 Brunswick St, Fitzroy

☏ 03-9417 3270

🚊 Light rail or tram from city up Collins St and along Brunswick St

Open: lunch Tue–Sat 1200–1500; dinner Tue–Sun 1800–2230

Reservations unnecessary

All credit cards accepted

Japanese

$$

More like a Japanese bistro than a sushi bar, this innovative little restaurant serves great – and good-value – sushi and *sashimi* plates. If you feel like being more adventurous, try pork belly accompanied by a sweet *miso* sauce or the delicate fish fillets.

Matteo's ⑦

533 Brunswick St, North Fitzroy

☏ 03-9481 1177

🚊 Light rail or tram from city up Collins St and along Brunswick St to North Fitzroy

Open: lunch Sun–Fri 1200–1430; dinner daily 1800–2200

Reservations recommended

All credit cards accepted

Mediterranean

$ $

Matteo's is an elegant, old-world restaurant serving some of the best modern Italian and Mediterranean food in Melbourne. There is a bold focus on serving seasonal Victorian produce such as Gippsland lamb, black mussels or Milawa soft sheeps' milk cheeses with modern Australian and Italian touches. The superb wine list changes monthly, with many wines available by the glass.

Vegetarian Orgasm [8]

117 Smith St, Fitzroy

03-9419 9321

No 86 tram along Smith St from Victoria Parade and city

Open: Mon–Fri 1200–1500, 1700–2200, Sat–Sun 1200–2200

Reservations unnecessary

All credit cards accepted

Vegetarian

$

Despite the irreverent name, this is a serious vegetarian restaurant. There is food here to suit the vegetarian, vegan or anyone with a food allergy, while even regular carnivores will find the quality and choices – and rich homemade (and vegan) desserts – tempting to the taste buds. Lunch times are more casual and breezy affairs.

Wild Yak [9]

97 Smith St, Fitzroy

03-9417 6661

No 86 tram along Smith St from Victoria Parade and the city centre

Open: Mon–Thu 1100–late, Fri–Sun 0900–late

Reservations unnecessary

Tibetan

$

What this functional restaurant lacks in décor, aesthetics and service, it more than compensates for with a tasty budget array of Tibetan food. Try the magnificent *dhal*, fried *momos*, steamed *tingmos* and many tofu dishes, which are especially good shared amongst a large table or group.

▲ Brunswick St festival

FITZROY: BRUNSWICK ST AND SMITH ST
Bars, cafés and pubs

Babka's Bakery Café 10
258 Brunswick St, Fitzroy
✆ 03-9416 0091

The bakery sends wonderful smells of baking out on to the street while the café tables are always filled with breakfasters or lunchers enjoying the cakes, breads and Russian specialities.

Black Cat Café 11
252 Brunswick St, Fitzroy
✆ 03-9419 6230

With its outdoor tables, mismatched chairs and excellent coffee and homemade cakes, this is a classic Brunswick St haunt, beloved of artists and ageing writers.

Carmen Bar 12
74 Johnston St, Fitzroy
✆ 03-9417 4794

This is one of the best of the numerous Spanish bars scattered along Johnston St, just north of Brunswick St, and is famous for its Spanish food, *Sol y Sombras* (a traditional drink mixing sambuca and cognac) and live flamenco dancers (Thu–Sat nights).

Gluttony – It's a Sin 13
278 Smith St, Collingwood
✆ 03-9416 0336

The place to visit if you are really hungry or definitely not calorie counting, for sinfully huge servings of everything from smoked salmon and caviar to Cajun barramundi, home-cooked muffins and some of the richest desserts in town.

The Grace Darling Hotel 14
114 Smith St, Collingwood
✆ 03-9416 0055

History was made in this solid bluestone pub when the Collingwood Football Club was founded in its cellars more than 100 years ago. Now its exterior hides a classy wine bar serving up-market salads, pies, sausages and steaks, while its light formal dining room cooks modern Australian restaurant fare.

Gypsy Bar 15
334 Brunswick St, Fitzroy
✆ 03-9419 0548

Coffee or lunch is on offer during the day, but this lively bar is best experienced in the early hours of the morning, whilst enjoying a cognac or a drambuie after the band has finished.

Jika Jika Hotel 16
5 Rae St, North Fitzroy
✆ 03-9489 1974

The ugly, blue-painted Jika Jika hides unpretentious **Rubira**'s restaurant in its back dining room, where seafood worshippers flock to experience perfectly cooked, fresh seafood-only feasts, and where sharing a platter of mixed entrées is often the best choice.

Mario's 17
303 Brunswick St, Fitzroy
✆ 03-9417 3343

This café is a breakfast favourite, for its affordable food, great scrambled eggs, welcoming waiters and the open windows looking out on to bustling Brunswick St.

The Night Cat 18
141 Johnston St, Fitzroy
✆ 03-9417 0090

A younger, hip crowd is attracted to this spacious, mirrored art-deco hall, complete with couches, three bars and constant live swing and jazz music.

De Oliveira's [19]

344 Nicholson St, Fitzroy
☏ 03-9419 1857

Now more a restaurant than a pub, with its opulent air and rooms filled with ornate mirrors and statues, the ever-changing European menu and specials board makes choosing between the delectable courses very difficult.

The Provincial Hotel [20]

299 Brunswick St, Fitzroy
☏ 03-9417 2228

This fine old Victorian hotel has set the pace with its modern European kitchen serving favourites from wood-fired pizzas and *calzone* to *confit du canard*, squid-ink spaghetti and some wonderful lamb shank specials. Dine in the airy atrium room, or outside in the courtyard, or sample the famous lemon and lime tarts at the bar or café.

Retro Café [21]

413 Brunswick St, Fitzroy
☏ 03-9419 9103

Some of the best coffee and breakfasts in town can be enjoyed at this lurid 1950s- and 1960s-revival venue, while its mix of Asian and modern Australian café food is popular throughout the day, as are its big windows, bright colours and indoor waterfall.

Robert Burns Hotel [22]

376 Smith St, Collingwood
☏ 03-9417 2233

This red-brick, unpretentious hotel houses Melbourne's best – and best-value – Spanish restaurant, where the jugs of *sangria* and huge plates of paella and *mariscada* are so popular that it is often booked up days in advance.

Ruby Bar [18]

299 Brunswick St, Fitzroy
☏ 03-9417 2228

Tucked away in a corner of the Provincial Hotel, this bar is the in-place for the cool, thirty-something late-night artistic crowd to share a glass of champagne over jazz.

Soul Food Café [23]

273 Smith St, Fitzroy
☏ 03-9419 2949

Enjoy massive main courses and great fruit smoothies in colourful and cosy surroundings.

Toast Café [24]

106 Smith St, Collingwood
☏ 03-9415 6882

Breakfast is more a gourmet feast here, with speciality sausages, eggs Florentine, 'magic' mushrooms and an array of toasted breads.

Vegie Bar [25]

380 Brunswick St, Fitzroy
☏ 03-9417 6935

This cavernous café serves huge plates of vegetarian food right through the day, from burritos, sushi rolls and *roti* wraps to great soups and (no-meat) burgers.

Yelza [10]

245 Gertrude St, Fitzroy
☏ 03-9416 2689

A relative newcomer to Fitzroy, Yelza is the perfect place to enjoy a quiet glass of wine or martini, with its red velvet wallpaper, stone fountains and great, good-value food.

▲ Gypsy Bar

FITZROY: BRUNSWICK ST AND SMITH ST

Shops, markets and picnic sites

Shops

An Apple A Day 26

194 Smith St, Collingwood
☏ 03-9419 2317

Freshly squeezed fruit juices, fruit salads and smoothies are fabulous here, while a full range of fresh fruit and vegetables can be bought from the back of the store.

Babka's Bakery 11

358 Brunswick St, Fitzroy
☏ 03-9416 0091

Stock up on picnic goodies such as bread, soft baguettes, rabbit pies, Danish pastries, rich cakes and wonderful tarts from this bakery-cum-café.

Bombay Bazaar 27

197 Brunswick St, Fitzroy
☏ 03-9417 2123

Indian delicacies such as Bombay duck (dried fish), fresh Indian spices, lentils, poppadoms and *ghee* abound in this enticing store.

Charmaine's Ice Cream Shop 6

370 Brunswick St, Fitzroy
☏ 03-9417 5379

Chocoholics and ice-cream fans will find their heart's delight at this shop where the chilli and chocolate mix is a hot favourite.

Jasper's 28

267 Brunswick St, Fitzroy
☏ 03-9416 0921

Jasper's is one of Melbourne's best-known coffee brands, and its 12 blends or 18 regional varieties from New Guinea to Africa can be bought – along with a plethora of coffee-making paraphernalia – from its Brunswick St retail outlet.

Jonathon's of Collingwood 29

122 Smith St, Collingwood
☏ 03-9419 4339

Jonathon Gianfreda is the butcher of choice to many of Melbourne's top chefs and restaurants, as well as its wealthy epicurean set. Over 25 years, he has developed his own personal suppliers for everything from rabbits, ducks and the best fillet steak to the special salt-bush-flavoured lamb; the homemade sausages and Gypsy ham are unsurpassed.

Kebab Factory 30

320–4 Brunswick St, Fitzroy
☏ 03-9419 5526

All the best in Turkish takeaway food is on offer here, from dips and Turkish bread to kebabs, falafels and Turkish Delight.

Maison de Tunisie 31

24 Smith St, Collingwood
☏ 03-9416 1385

You will find all your Tunisian and Moroccan favourites stocked here, from couscous and blisteringly hot *harissa* to olives, *glacé* fruit, dates and even rose petals mixed with spices.

Mamma Vittoria Pasta Classica 32

343 Smith St, Fitzroy
☏ 03-9417 5414

This shop is noted for its fresh pasta such as *gnocchi*, tortellini, *agnolotti* and the house speciality of filled pasta *bon-bons*.

The Organic Warehouse 33

112 Argyle St, Fitzroy
☏ 03-9415 9942

This popular vegetarian café also sells organic

Organic Wholefoods 34

277 Smith St, Fitzroy
☎ 03-9419 5347

A mecca for organic foodstuffs, which sells everything from organic fruit and vegetables to yoghurts, tofu and muesli mixes.

Simon Johnson Fine Foods 35

12–14 St David St, Fitzroy
☎ 03-9486 9456

The staff are extraordinarily well informed and helpful in this warehouse devoted to all that is best in the world's food, tucked away off Brunswick St. This is the place to buy everything from olive oil and polenta to smoked salmon, Spanish saffron, homemade stocks and Beluga caviar – all from the best producers both locally and internationally.

Sword's 36

133 Brunswick St, Fitzroy
☎ 03-9415 1122

Wine drinkers are not neglected at Sword's, where more than a dozen Australian wines are available to be tasted, bought in bulk or in the easily recognisable one-litre glass swing-top bottles.

and vegan pies, pastries and flours – and reflexology courses!

Tea Too (T2) 11

340 Brunswick St, Fitzroy
☎ 03-9417 3722

This classic tea house is a wonder to visit, sniff and taste, with more than 200 varieties of tea from around the world on offer, all beautifully stored in jars, little drawers and wooden boxes.

The Upper Crust 37

206 Smith St, Collingwood
☎ 03-9415 9511

Try this bakery for all your favourite brands of bread, bagels, muffins and pastries.

▲ Tea Too

Little Vietnam

Taste of Asia

Walk down Richmond's Victoria St in the early evening or on a Saturday and you are suddenly transported to the bustling, madcap lanes and streets of Ho Chi Minh City (Saigon) or Hanoi. All around are Vietnamese voices, signs in Chinese and Vietnamese characters and wall-to-wall grocery shops, butchers, fish shops, vegetable stores, soup bars and noisy cheap restaurants, selling and serving the most delicious and tasty Vietnamese delicacies and meals it is possible to imagine.

One of the cheapest and most simple restaurants in Little Vietnam is **Dong Ba 2** (*258B Victoria St, Richmond; ∅ 03-9427 9099;* ⓟ *No 42 Mont Albert tram from Collins St in the CBD; open: daily 0930–2130; reservations unnecessary; no credit cards accepted;* ❸), where most of the diners are Vietnamese locals eating their quick standard dinner. Don't expect elegant décor – this is a basic Vietnamese with fluorescent lights and bare tables – but it is a cheap, friendly restaurant specialising in the hearty noodle soups (*bun*), flavoured with spices such as lemongrass and more complex ingredients, which come from the old Vietnamese royal capital of Hue. *Bun Bo Hue* (Hue beef noodle soup) is the staple meal here, but plenty of other Vietnamese delicacies are served as well – just ask the friendly owner.

Further up Victoria St is one of the area's most popular Vietnamese restaurants, **Thy Thy 1** (*Level 1, 142 Victoria St, Richmond; ∅ 03-94279 1104;* ⓟ *No 42 Mont Albert tram from Collins St in the CBD; open: daily 0800–2200; reservations unnecessary; no credit cards accepted;* ❸). Upstairs, under dingy lighting, and eating off closely packed, paper-covered tables, is a crowd varying from students to well-heeled families and Vietnamese locals, all there for the noise, the crush, the great fresh yet budget-cheap food and the quick service.

Just down the street is **Quan 88** (which literally means 'Shop

88') (*88 Victoria St, Richmond; ✆ 03-9428 6850;* 🚊 *No 42 Mont Albert tram from Collins St in the CBD; open: Sun-Thu 1000-2200, Fri-Sat 1000-2300; reservations recommended; all credit cards accepted;* ❸), serving some of the best southern Vietnamese food. Most famous are its generous main courses of spicy quail, salted squid flavoured with star anise, grilled beef in mint leaves and flaming pork with Cantonese sauce. For starters, the spring rolls and rice paper rolls are hard to beat, although the cold rare beef salad with lemon juice and chilli is irresistible.

Across Victoria St, in a converted historic Australian pub, **Minh Tan 3** (*397 Victoria St, Richmond; ✆ 03-9428 0504;* 🚊 *No 42 Mont Albert tram from Collins St in the CBD; open: Sun-Thu 1100-0100, Fri-Sat 1100-0200; reservations recommended;* 💳 VISA; ❸) is the third restaurant in the family Minh Tan dynasty of Victoria St. Slightly more formal (it has white tablecloths), gracious, slow moving and a little more expensive than other Vietnamese restaurants in the strip, Minh Tan 3 is the perfect place to bring a family group or a guest from overseas who wants to experience authentic Vietnamese food. This restaurant, with its large wall tanks filled with fresh (and live) fish, crabs and crays, specialises in seafood from south Vietnam – its house speciality is the wonderful steamed crab with beer sauce – but also serves a mixture of other Vietnamese and Chinese favourites.

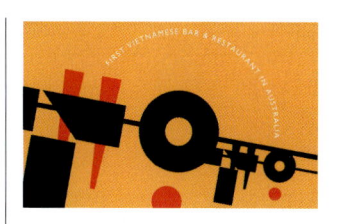

For the ultimate in Vietnamese yuppie chic, cross Victoria St again to reach **Tho Tho Bar and Restaurant** (*60-6 Victoria St, Richmond; ✆ 03-9428 2036;* 🚊 *No 42 Mont Albert tram from Collins St in the CBD; open: daily 1100-2400; reservations unnecessary; all credit cards accepted;* ❸). Describing itself as the first Vietnamese bar in Victoria St, Tho Tho is more like a hip modern Australian bistro: retro coloured designer tables and chairs have replaced the bare globes and laminated tables. Its vast restaurant space is always full – of both people and noise – service is rapid if graceless, and the food is both cheap and fresh. The spring rolls wrapped in lettuce leaves and Vietnamese mint, the rice-paper rolls and the salty squid are all as good here as anywhere in the street. A speciality of the house is its Dalat-style hotpot cooking, especially its delicious seafood hotpot.

> ... hearty noodle soups or 'bun', flavoured with spices such as lemongrass and more complex ingredients ...

Little Vietnam | 67

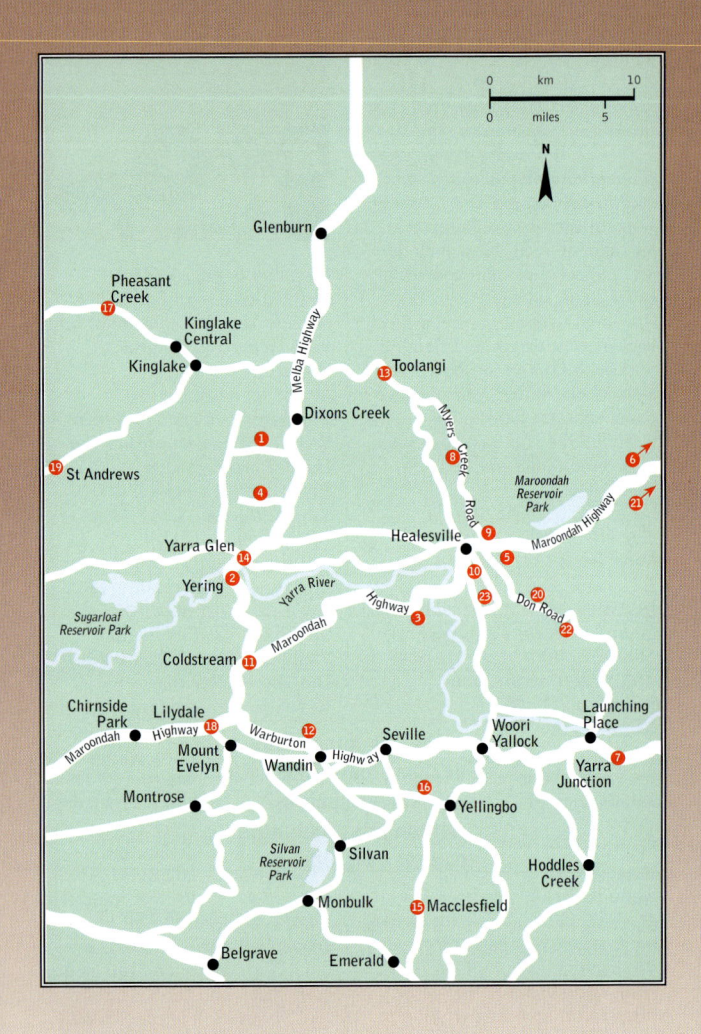

The Yarra Valley

Not all of Melbourne's best restaurants are to be found in the city. Why not enjoy a weekend in the country, only just over an hour's drive outside Melbourne in the Yarra Valley, savouring some of the country's best wines, as well as its wonderful food.

THE YARRA VALLEY
Restaurants

De Bortoli Winery Restaurant ❶

Pinnacle La., Dixons Creek

☏ 03-5965 2271

Between Lilydale and Healesville turn north on the Melba Hwy, drive through Yarra Glen and take the second major turn left on Pinnacle La.

Open: lunch daily 1200–1500, dinner daily from 1900

Reservations recommended

All credit cards accepted

Northern Italian

$$

This family-owned restaurant, built on a picturesque hillside elevated above the family vineyards, positively reeks of Tuscany, northern Italy and all the good things in life. Specialities include the *antipasto*, homemade potato *gnocchi* and squid-ink pasta, plus local venison and trout. De Bortoli wines, including the well-known Gulf Station and Windy Peak labels, can be tasted for free in the cellars beneath the restaurant.

Eleonore's at Château Yering ❷

Melba Hwy, Yering (near Yarra Glen)

☏ 03-9237 3333

Between Lilydale and Healesville, turn north on the Melba Hwy towards Yarra Glen; after about 8km Château Yering is on the right

Open: lunch Fri–Sun from 1200, dinner daily from 1830–late

Reservations essential

All credit cards accepted

Modern Australian

$$$

Château Yering unashamedly combines fine modern Australian food with an opulent romantic setting. The château was the first grand building to be built in the Yarra Valley in 1854 and at Eleonore's – named after the sophisticated Swiss mother of the château's creator – you can enjoy delicacies such as Yarra Valley venison, pigeon pie, crayfish tortellini or white rabbit saddle.

Eyton on Yarra ❸

Corner of Maroondah Hwy and Hill Rd, Coldstream

☏ 03-5962 2119

On the Maroondah Hwy pass through Lilydale and turn off to the right before Healesville

Open: lunch daily 1200–1500

Reservations recommended

All credit cards accepted

Modern Australian

$$

Enjoy a casual, easy-style lunch in this light and airy restaurant with the vaulted ceilings and views out over the winery's lake and surrounding vineyards. Specialising in operatic and classical music concerts, Eyton on Yarra's restaurant has many fans. This is the place to drop in for lunch and enjoy stylish food such as local roast duck with quince or crisp-skinned salmon, or just to savour a glass of chilled white wine with cheese on the outdoor terrace.

Fergusson Winery Restaurant ❹

Wills Rd, Yarra Glen

☏ 03-5965 2237

Between Lilydale and Healesville turn north on the Melba Hwy, drive through Yarra Glen and take the first major turn left on Wills Rd

Open: lunch daily 1200–1500, dinner Fri–Sat from 1800

Reservations recommended

All credit cards accepted

Rustic Australian

$$

This long-running popular restaurant in the Yarra Valley mixes rustic good cheer, chunky wooden tables

▲ De Bortoli Winery Restaurant

Riberry Café and Restaurant 7

2473 Warburton Hwy, Yarra Junction

☎ 03-5967 2095

On the Maroondah Hwy pass through Lilydale and turn right on to the Warburton Hwy to reach Yarra Junction

Open: lunch Thu–Sat 1100–1600, Sun 1200–1700; dinner Fri–Sat 1800–2100

Reservations recommended

Modern Australian

The upper end of the Yarra Valley amidst the tall forests and lyrebird ferny creeks has long been deprived of good eateries, so the opening of the new Riberry Restaurant has been a welcome addition to Yarra Junction. Enjoy local Yellingbo yabbies, Healesville pasta, and valley nuts and berries, as well as local trout risotto, game pies and glazed duck on potato pancakes.

and a slate floor, with an atmosphere of wine, song and friendliness. Spit-roasted beef, carved by owner Peter Fergusson, mixed with a Fergusson Shiraz is hard to beat.

Healesville Restaurant and Café 5

434 Maroondah Hwy, Healesville

☎ 03-5962 1300

On the Maroondah Hwy pass through Lilydale, the restaurant is on the far side of Healesville

Open: Thu–Sun lunch from 1200, dinner from 1830

Reservations unnecessary

All credit cards accepted

Modern Australian

Drop in to this casual place for a light lunch of *focaccia*, soup or a Yarra Valley *antipasto* platter, or for dinner with its rice-paper rolls, goats' cheese tarts and heavenly saffron angel-hair pasta made by the **Yarra Valley Pasta Shop** down the road. Don't miss desserts made from local hazelnuts, cream and berries.

Marylands Country House 6

22 Falls Rd, Marysville

☎ 03-5963 3204

On the Maroondah Hwy pass through Lilydale and Healesville before reaching Marysville

Open: lunch Sun 1230–1430, dinner daily from 1830

Reservations recommended

All credit cards accepted

Modern Australian

This large mock-Tudor hotel, surrounded by the waterfalls and tall dark forests of Yarra Ranges National Park, has an air of English gentility, old-fashioned tennis parties and healthy walking weekends. The contemporary menu of seafood, beef, lamb and local game involves interesting sauces, *jus* and accompanying chutneys.

Strathvea 8

Myers Creek Rd, Healesville

☎ 03-5962 4109

Maroondah Hwy to Healesville, turn left up Myers Creek Rd and drive through tall mountain ash forest and ferns for 10 minutes before reaching Strathvea

Open: daily for dinner with reservations

Reservations essential – reservations only

Home cooking

70 | The Yarra Valley

Strathvea is a charming 1920s guesthouse set amidst two hectares of beautiful rhododendron and azalea gardens with views out to the surrounding Yarra Valley and mountain forest ranges. Fine home cooking is served up in the homestead-style dining room. Restaurant bookings for the fixed-price dinner can be made by visitors not staying at the guesthouse.

The Yarra Glen Grand Hotel ❷

Melba Hwy, Yering (near Yarra Glen)

✆ 03-9237 3333

🚗 On the Maroondah Hwy pass through Lilydale; between Lilydale and Healesville, turn north on the Melba Hwy to Yarra Glen

Open: Grand Dining Room Tue–Sat from 1900; bistro and veranda café daily 1200–1430, 1800–2030

Reservations essential for Grand Dining Room but unnecessary for bistro and café

All credit cards accepted

Modern Australian

$$$

The 1888 Yarra Glen Grand Hotel is an imposing edifice which looks out over the vineyards and rich river flats of the Yarra Valley from its place in the centre of the little Yarra Glen town. Its cosy and historic Grand Dining Room specialises in fixed-price dinner featuring regional favourites such as rack of lamb, herb-crusted Yarra Valley salmon and peppered kangaroo fillets.

Yering Station Restaurant and Wine Bar ❷

38 Melba Hwy, Yering (near Yarra Glen)

✆ 03-9730 1107

🚗 On the Maroondah Hwy pass through Lilydale; between Lilydale and Healesville, turn north on the Melba Hwy towards Yarra Glen; about 8km later Yering Station is on the right

Open: daily 1000–1800

Reservations recommended

All credit cards accepted

Modern Australian

$$

Yering Station Wine Bar and casual restaurant is located in an elegant and soaring new building made of local sandstone and glass, overlooking the historic vineyards of Yering Station and blue Yarra Ranges beyond. This is the place to enjoy a relaxed but stylish lunch, either in the sun on the terrace or warmed inside by the light-filled room. The menu changes seasonally, with many of the fresh ingredients such as pasta, trout, berries, cheeses, game and vegetables sourced locally and cooked in a contemporary Australian style with touches of Asian and Middle-Eastern influences. The fresh oysters with a *verjuice* dressing, accompanied by Yering Station's Yarrabank sparkling Cuvée, are irresistible.

▲ The Yarra Glen Grand Hotel

THE YARRA VALLEY
Bars, cafés and pubs

Black Spur Nursery and Tea House ❾

349–53 Maroondah Hwy, Healesville

☏ 03-5962 6045

The Black Spur Nursery and Tea House is a sunny, glass-surrounded tea house amidst its flowers and ferns, where a blackboard tells the story of what light delights, such as warm chicken salad, pumpkin soup or quiches, are on the day's menu, as well as its all-day coffee, tea and cakes.

Church St Gallery and Café ❿

4 Church St, Healesville

☏ 03-5962 2117

The Church St Gallery and Café serves coffee and home-cooked afternoon teas amongst contemporary artwork in the high-arched heritage building that was once the old Mechanics Institute.

Domain Chandon ⓫

Green Point vineyards, Maroondah Hwy, Coldstream

☏ 03-9739 1110

A highlight for most visitors to the Yarra Valley is always the tasting room of Domain Chandon, owned by legendary French champagne makers Moët et Chandon. Domain Chandon makes magnificent sparkling wines, Cuvées, Chardonnays and sparkling Pinot Noirs, sold overseas under their alternative name, Green Point. On tours of the winery you can sip glasses of Chandon's Brut Rosé and Brut de Noir accompanied by locally made trout pâté.

The Healesville Hotel ❿

256 Maroondah Hwy, Healesville

☏ 03-5962 4002

Local pubs are few and far between in the Yarra Valley and only The Healesville Hotel with its solid façade and high-ceiling dining room has made an effort to replace its stodgy counter teas with creative, interesting modern Australian food suited to the more sophisticated city palate. Here you may find Yarra Valley venison and mushroom pie, pasta from Healesville or local beef fillet or fresh salmon, all served with flair.

Martha's Tea Room ⓬

Mont de Lancey, Wellington Rd, Wandin North

☏ 03-5964 2088

In the cherry and berry town of Wandin the historic pioneer homestead of Mont de Lancey has been restored by the local community and is now open to the public, where Martha's Tea Room serves delicious berries and cream, Devonshire teas, homemade cakes and light lunches in the old 1920s milking shed.

Singing Gardens Tea Rooms ⓭

Arden, Toolangi

☏ 03-5962 9282

North of Healesville in the forests of tiny Toolangi is the mountain home of early Australian poet and 'Sentimental Bloke', C.J. Dennis. The 'singing gardens' of Arden, with their masses of European trees, rhododendrons, daffodils and semi-formal shrubs, are open to the public, while Devonshire tea in the Singing Gardens Tea Rooms in the mountain air makes a well-deserved treat.

Sweetwater Café ❷

Château Yering, Melba Hwy, Yering

☏ 03-9237 3333

At the five-star Château Yering luxury hotel (*see page 69*), Sweetwater

Café is both a relaxing drop-in café and a gracious place to have an informal, but top-class lunch. Sweetwater was the name of the first grape variety planted in the Yarra Valley in the 1850s, and the popular Sweetwater Café (book ahead) looks like it is set to stay too.

Yarra Glen Café and Store 14

36 Bell St, Yarra Glen
✆ 03-9730 1122

At Yarra Glen, just opposite the Grand Hotel, an old 1840s farm cottage has been converted into the warm and homely Yarra Glen Café and Store where good-value and filling sandwiches, *antipasto* platters, soups, tarts, game sausages, *bruschetta* and puddings are sold for lunch, as well as hearty breakfasts and an array of local produce.

Yarra Valley Dairy 2

McMeikan's Rd, Yering
✆ 03-9739 0023

An unforgettable experience is lunch at the Yarra Valley Dairy, set in a 100-year-old corrugated iron shed containing a working dairy. More than 200 cows and a herd of goats are milked daily, and magnificent French and Italian-style exotic cheeses (mainly soft cheeses) are hand-produced in its specially built boutique cheese factory. There is also a rustic licensed restaurant tucked away under the wooden beams, serving great platters of cheese, breads and other simple local foods; try the *dégustation* platter, accompanied by a glass of local red wine, as the cows wander past the window outside.

Yarra Valley Pasta Shop and Café 9

325 Maroondah Hwy, Healesville
✆ 03-5962 1888

Maria Colaneri and her daughter Lisa serve the best coffee in the Yarra Valley and casual Italian pasta lunches to die for. The big paper sheet menu on the sunflower-coloured walls tells lunchers what fresh pasta Maria has cooked that day; it may be their special squid-ink angel-hair pasta tossed with an assortment of seafood, or free-range egg *tagliatelle* with smoked chicken or their famous ricotta *gnochetti* with basil pesto and cream.

▲ Domain Chandon

THE YARRA VALLEY
Shops, markets and picnic sites

Shops

Australian Rainbow Trout Farm 15

26 Mulhall's Rd, Macclesfield
☏ 03-5968 4711

At the Australian Rainbow Trout Farm you can catch trout yourself in a picnic setting or buy fresh trout, smoked trout or trout pâté for instant eating.

Gateway Bakers 11

Shop 2, North Gateway, Coldstream
☏ 03-9739 1233

Tucked away in Coldstream is Gateway Bakers, a real Scottish bakery that makes magical soft and milky Scottish loaves and great oatcakes.

Gourmet Yabby Farm 16

Beltana Park, 185 Beenak Rd, Yellingbo
☏ 03-5964 8265

Catch your own yabbies and native blackfish (or buy them fresh or frozen if you prefer) at the Gourmet Yabby Farm, where barbecue and picnic facilities are available, as well as tours of the hydroponic roses and tomatoes.

Kennedy and Wilson Chocolate Shop 9

321 Maroondah Hwy, Healesville
☏ 03-5964 9549

Former winemaker Peter Wilson has turned his culinary skills and tastebuds to making the finest, most luxurious chocolates possible. His rich and exquisite handmade K&W chocolates are stocked by only Australia's top gourmet retailers.

Kinglake Raspberries 17

Tooheys Rd, Pheasant Creek
☏ 03-5786 5360

Kinglake Raspberries is Victoria's largest pick-your-own raspberry farm, where the public can pick raspberries by the punnet from the paddock, as well as buy the full range of local berry jams and preserves.

Lilydale Apiaries 18

213–23 Lilydale–Montrose Rd, Lilydale
☏ 03-9736 2722

Local honey made from grey box, clover, orange blossom and some of the mountains' flowering gums can be bought at Lilydale Apiaries.

Lilydale Herb Farm 18

61 Mangans Rd, Lilydale
☏ 03-9739 6899

The full range of its medicinal and cooking herbs, both fresh and dried, as well as aromatherapy oils and scents, are sold at this nursery and gift shop.

Maroondah Orchards 11

713–19 Maroondah Hwy, Coldstream
☏ 03-9739 1041

Homemade fruit juice and a range of fresh fruit in season, from peaches, pears, apples and nectarines to *nashi* fruit and cherries, is sold in an outdoor shed.

Yarra Glen Bakehouse 14

30 Bell St, Yarra Glen
☏ 03-9730 1873

For bread, the Yarra Glen Bakehouse makes a good selection of breads, breadsticks, rolls, pies and cakes.

Yarra Valley Dairy 2

McMeikan's Rd, Yering
☏ 03-9739 0023

Cheeses galore can be bought and sampled at the Yarra Valley Dairy where freshly made soft cheeses such as Persian feta, ashed goats' milk pyramids, *grabbetto* cones, fromage frais blue *torte* and washed-rind cows' milk cheese form the basis of any great picnic.

Yarra Valley Pasta Shop ❾

325 Maroondah Hwy, Healesville
✆ 03-5962 1888

This is where serious gourmands and restaurateurs come from across Melbourne to buy Maria Colaneri's fresh-cut pasta, such as its herb garden *fettuccine*, squid-ink angel-hair pasta, handmade ravioli stuffed with local Buxton smoked trout and Yarra Valley goats' cheese, cannelloni, lasagne and saffron spaghetti. It all lies temptingly in neat airing drawers or out on display.

Markets

St Andrews Market ⓳

Heidelberg–Kinglake Rd
Open: every Sat 0800–1300

The large and sprawling St Andrews Market majors in organic fruit and vegetables, alternative lifestyles and New Age crafts.

Yarra Glen Craft Market ⓮

Yarra Glen Racecourse
Open: Oct–Jun, first Sun each month 0900–1400

More than 300 stalls sell local crafts, plants, foods and produce.

Yarra Valley Regional Farmers' Market ❷

On the third Sunday of each month this market is held in the old barn at Yering Station and is an occasion not to be missed as local producers sell their deliciously fresh wares in an historic setting.

Picnic sites

Badger Weir Reserve ⓴

Visit the lovely cool and ferny Badger Weir Reserve, just out from Healesville.

Black Spur ㉑

The Black Spur picnic grounds are surrounded by tall mountain ash forest on the Maroondah Highway between Healesville and Marysville.

Don Road ㉒

Drive along the spectacular Don Road, with its golden wattles and views as it travels the ridge between Healesville and Launching Place.

Healesville Sanctuary ㉓

Picnic within the grounds of the beloved Healesville Sanctuary with its abundant native animal displays (watch out for hungry emus).

▲ Yarra Valley Pasta Shop

The Yarra Valley | 75

Victorian wines

A viticulturist's paradise

Australia's wine industry has been booming for the past decade, with its wines winning top awards worldwide, its young progressive winemakers employed across the globe, and an incredibly healthy export wine industry. The golden, cool climate of Victoria makes it a viticulturist's paradise – the first vines were planted on the rolling hills around Melbourne in the 1860s and, by 1889, a Château Yering wine from the Yarra Valley had won the Grand Prix wine prize at the Paris exhibition. By the turn of the century, a change in drinking habits and a severe outbreak of the vine disease phylloxera saw the industry fall into decline, and it was not until the 1970s that Victorian wines enjoyed a massive resurgence in popularity, numbers and production that still continues today.

There are five main wine-growing areas in Victoria today: the **Yarra Valley**, the cool northeast region of Victoria around **Rutherglen and Milawa**, the **Mornington Peninsula** on the eastern side of Port Phillip Bay, the **central Pyrenees** and the flat, irrigated plains of the mighty **Murray River** around Mildura in the northwest. The time of grape harvest varies, depending on the climate in each region and grape varieties grown, but is usually in full swing in all areas in the months between March and May.

Wine tasting and wine touring through some of the major wine-growing districts is almost a national hobby. Almost all of the wineries, from the largest corporate-owned establishments to the smallest boutique winery, are open daily for tastings and cellar-door sales of new vintages. Most wineries will also ship wines overseas or have agents abroad, so it is not usually necessary to have to carry away with you any wine you purchase.

Given Victoria's Mediterranean, hot-summer, winter-rainfall climate, most vineyards can grow myriad grape varieties and are unconstrained by the regional conventions of old wine-making countries such as France and Italy. However, some wine types are becoming better associated with Victorian regions, and even specific wineries, than others. **Rutherglen** is best known for its full-bodied and big 'Rutherglen Reds' such as

Cabernet Sauvignons from century-old wineries such as **Campbells** and **Chambers**. But it is its fortified muscats, tokays and ports from both Rutherglen and Glenrowan that are even more internationally renowned, with **Bullers**, **Morris**, **All Saints** and **Bailey's** among the best. The cooler climate of wines grown around **Whitfield** and **Milawa** closer to the mountains makes for crisper whites and lighter, softer reds, with **Brown Brothers** winery renowned for its adventurous approach to experimenting with new varieties untried by other vineyards.

Around Melbourne, vineyards proliferate in the beautiful **Yarra Valley**, between Red Hill and Flinders on the Mornington Peninsula, at the foot of Mt Macedon and on the Bellarine Peninsula between Anakie and Drysdale. Chardonnays, sparkling wine and light reds are best from the Yarra Valley, Pinot Noirs from the Mornington Peninsula, and powerful Shiraz and crisp Sauvignon Blanc from the Central Victoria and Geelong region. In the Yarra Valley, taste sparkling wine at the French-owned **Domain Chandon** (*see page 72*), plus the full range of locally made wines at **Yering Station**'s historic tasting cellars (*see page 71*), award-winning red wines at **De Bortoli** (*see page 69*) and an excellent Pinot Noir at **Coldstream Hills**.

On the **Mornington Peninsula** grapes sprawl in green abundance amongst its rolling hills between Dromana, Main Ridge, Red Hill and Balnarring, flanked by the two bays of Westernport and Port Phillip. They produce fresh, full-flavoured wines with gentle tannins; the Pinot Noirs such as **Stonier's** from Merricks and from **Tuck's Ridge** at Red Hill are especially superb, although in recent years Chardonnays from **Willow Creek** have also won top awards.

In central Victoria, between Seymour and Nagambie, the **Mitchelton** winery alongside the lazy Goulburn River has superb white and red wines, while just downstream the historic **Château Tahbilk**, with its strong red wines and historic underground cellars, is another winery not to be missed. Near Ararat and Stawell in western Victoria is the hamlet of Great Western, famous as home of the **Seppelt**'s champagne cellars, with the boutique **Best's** winery nearby well known for its red wines.

Wine festivals are another major activity across Victoria, often combined with music, opera and jazz performances, or with local food festivals. The big events start in March with the **Yarra Valley Grape Grazing Festival**, followed by the classical **Musica Viva** festival at Domaine Chandon in April. The long Queen's Birthday weekend in June is the madcap **Mornington Peninsula Wine Weekend**, while as the sun arrives in November, **Rutherglen** warms up for its own wine weekend.

> **Wine tasting and wine touring through some of the major wine-growing districts is almost a national hobby.**

Around Port Phillip Bay

Melbourne's Port Phillip Bay provides a seaside playground that Melburnians treat as their own weekend and summer holiday retreat. Among other things, visit the Red Hill wineries, admire the little boats bobbing on the gentle seas at Blairgowrie, and take a coffee amongst the historic sandstone buildings and cafés that line Sorrento's main street.

AROUND PORT PHILLIP BAY
Restaurants

Arthurs ❶

Arthurs Seat Scenic Rd, Arthurs Seat

☎ 03-5981 4444

Drive to Dromana from Melbourne on the Nepean Hwy and Mornington Peninsula Freeway, turn left up the steep and winding Arthurs Seat Rd to the top of the hill; alternatively, take the spectacular chairlift from the foot of Arthurs Seat

Open: Dec–Feb lunch Wed–Sun from 1200, dinner Wed–Sat from 1830; rest of the year lunch Sat–Sun from 1200, dinner Fri–Sat from 1830

Reservations essential

All credit cards accepted

Modern Australian

$$

The view from Arthurs Restaurant at the peak of Arthurs Seat is magnificent; the sweep of the Mornington Peninsula and Port Phillip Bay is spread out below. Fortunately, the food often earns as many superlatives as the view, with the Swiss chef and owner, Hermann Schneider, a highly regarded perfectionist serving delicate seasonal food.

The Baths ❷

3278 Point Nepean Rd, Sorrento

☎ 03-5984 1500

Drive to Sorrento from Melbourne on the Nepean Hwy and Mornington Peninsula Freeway, or by car or passenger ferry from Queenscliff to Sorrento pier

Open: Fri–Sat 0800–0100, Sun–Thu 0800–2300

Reservations recommended

All credit cards accepted

78 | Around Port Phillip Bay

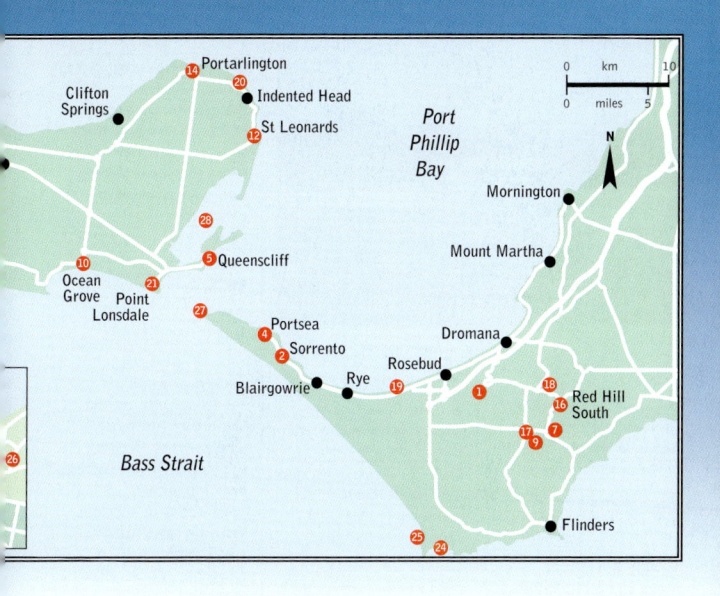

Modern Mediterranean-Asian
❸ $

This light, timber restaurant built out over the sands of Sorrento front beach, with the blue seas bobbing at its front steps, has one of the best locations of any restaurant in Victoria. Built in the old Sorrento tearooms, it is both casual yet classy, serving anything from breakfast and coffee to a sunset glass of wine accompanied by sushi or a breezy dinner of red chicken curries, stir-fried chicken with Hokkien noodles, Cantonese-style duck breast, or a platter of 'Japanese delights'.

The Beach House ❸

Eastern Beach Reserve, Geelong
✆ 03-5221 8322
🚗 Drive from central Melbourne over the Westgate Bridge on the Geelong (Princes) Freeway, and head to the east end of Geelong's Corio Bay waterfront; country trains to Geelong leave hourly from Melbourne's Spencer St Station

Open: daily 1200–1500, 1800–late
Reservations recommended
All credit cards accepted
Seafood-Mediterranean
❸ $

In 1993 Geelong's lovely timber art-deco Eastern Beach bathing pool and its attached Bathing Pavilion were restored, and the women's changing room on the first floor overlooking Corio Bay became the stylish Beach House Restaurant. The menu changes regularly and features seasonal local fish and mussels, as well as duck, steak and chicken delicacies, risottos and vegetarian fare.

Castle Restaurant at Peppers Delgany ❹

Point Nepean Rd, Portsea
✆ 03-5984 4000

Around Port Phillip Bay | 79

▲ The Baths

◉ Drive to Portsea from Melbourne on the Nepean Hwy and Mornington Peninsula Freeway, or by car or passenger ferry from Queenscliff via Sorrento

Open: daily, breakfast, lunch and dinner 0700–2400

Reservations essential

All credit cards accepted

Modern Australian

❸❸❸

A fake castle setting complete with rose garden and manicured lawns sounds a tad bizarre amidst the ti-tree and casuarina bush of the Portsea sand dunes where Melbourne's new money and old gentry own the millionaire cliff-top holiday houses. But the Castle Restaurant at Peppers Delgany overcomes the faux touch with its dignified, elegant, beautifully prepared food, earning itself gourmet status as one of Melbourne's best out-of-town restaurants.

Harry's ❺

Princess Park, Queenscliff

✆ 03-5258 3750

◉ Drive to Geelong and take the Bellarine Hwy leading to Queenscliff

Open: Dec–Feb daily 1230–1500, 1900–late; rest of year lunch Fri–Sun 1230–1500, dinner Thu–Sun 1900–late

Reservations recommended

All credit cards accepted

Seafood

❸❸

This little restaurant under the pine trees in the park by the old Queenscliff pier looks from the road as though it is located in an ugly red brick toilet block. Actually, it's an old bathing pavilion and its appearance is deceiving; it hides a restaurant serving marvellous seafood, situated almost right on the beach. Diners are served Portarlington fresh mussels and saffron pasta with blue swimmer crab as the ships and yachts glide past.

Koaki Restaurant ❻

Rippleside Park, Bell Parade, Geelong

✆ 03-5272 1925

◉ Drive from central Melbourne over the Westgate Bridge on the Geelong (Princes) Freeway, turn left down Bell Parade as the city centre draws near, before turning left again into a bayside park

Open: Tue–Sun 1800–2200

Reservations recommended

American Express

Japanese

❸❸

Tucked away in a suburban park on the Corio Bay foreshore, just north of Geelong city centre, is one of the best Japanese restaurants in Victoria. With its own Tokyo sushi master in residence, Koaki serves exemplary sushi, *sashimi* and *sukiyaki*.

Lime Restaurant ❷

3183 Point Nepean Rd, Sorrento

✆ 03-5984 4444

◉ Drive to Sorrento from Melbourne on the Nepean Hwy and Mornington Peninsula Freeway, or by car or passenger ferry from Queenscliff to Sorrento Pier

Open: Dec–Feb and Easter daily breakfast, lunch and dinner 0800–late; rest of the year Mon–Fri dinner from 1900, Sat–Sun breakfast, lunch and dinner 0800–2300

Reservations recommended

All credit cards accepted

Modern Australian

❸❸

This little restaurant in an old limestone cottage, opposite the

80 | Around Port Phillip Bay

golden beach and bobbing couta boats of the Sorrento Sailing Club, has a casual, holiday air yet serves classy modern food, including baked sardines, crab *tortellone*, and a hearty chargrilled Gippsland rump steak in a rich Shiraz sauce. Living up to its name, lime tarts, lime soufflés and lime ice cream are specialities.

Max's at Red Hill Estate ❼

Red Hill Estate Winery, 53 Red Hill–Shoreham Rd, Red Hill South

⌀ 03-5931 0177

🅟 Drive from Melbourne on the Nepean Hwy and Mornington Peninsula Freeway and take the Red Hill exit

Open: lunch daily from 1200, dinner Thu–Sat from 1900

Reservations recommended

All credit cards accepted

Mediterranean

$ $

At Max's restaurant the Mediterranean menu has been matched with suggested glasses of Red Hill Estate wines. Hard to go past is the entrée of King Island smoked salmon served on a cottage cheese blini accompanied by a Pinot Noir, or the King prawns seared in rosemary-and-garlic-infused olive oil and tossed with homemade pasta, accompanied by an unoaked Red Hill Estate Chardonnay.

Mietta's ❺

Queenscliff Hotel, 16 Gellibrand St, Queenscliff

⌀ 03-5258 1066

🅟 Drive to Geelong and take the Bellarine Hwy leading to the seaside resort town of Queenscliff, or take the car or passenger ferry from Sorrento

Open: dining room Wed–Sun 1900–2130; bistro daily 1200–1430, 1900–2100

Reservations essential

All credit cards accepted

Modern Australian

$ $ $

If looking for a special weekend away, with magnificent food enjoyed in 19th-century seaside grandeur, and expense is not really an issue, then Mietta's at the Queenscliff Hotel is hard to beat. Dinner served in the magnificently restored dining room is a set-price, three-course (plus appetisers and sorbets) extravaganza. But, for the more less financially affluent, a casual champagne on the terrace of the Queenscliff Hotel looking out over the sea, followed by a well-priced bar dinner of *gnocchi*, vegetarian lasagne or fresh fish comes close enough to the real Mietta's to satisfy many.

Sempre Caffe e Paninoteca ❽

88 Little Malop St, Geelong

⌀ 03-5229 8845

🅟 Drive from central Melbourne over the Westgate Bridge on the Geelong (Princes) Freeway to the central city, where Little Malop St is tucked behind the main shopping stretch

Open: Mon 1030–1600, Tue–Sat 1030–0100

Reservations recommended

American Express

Italian

$

Sempre Caffe e Paninoteca's food is contemporary Italian and its style chic; with its table lamps, attached grocery store and intimate atmosphere, it owes more to Chapel St, South Yarra than its Geelong heritage. Excellent risottos and lamb shanks, while the coffee is the best to be found in Geelong.

▲ Scallops at Harry's

AROUND PORT PHILLIP BAY
Bars, cafés and pubs

La Baracca Trattoria ❾

T'Gallant Winery,
Mornington–Flinders Rd,
Main Ridge
✆ 03-5989 6565

Meaning 'the shed' in Italian, this rustic little restaurant is literally built in an open tin shed next to the wine-making rooms, but its wooden tables are always full of relaxed, noisy crowds enjoying the fine wine, the hearty Umbrian food and the vineyard views.

Café Pelican ❷

2 St Aubins Way, Sorrento
✆ 03-5984 4478

For glittering calm bay views and a place for the kids to play on the sand while the parents enjoy a quiet breakfast and coffee, Café Pelican is unbeatable. Its waiters will even serve you breakfast on the sand, although a light lunch and crisp glass of cool white wine is even more attractive.

Continental Café ❷

1–21 Ocean Beach Rd, Sorrento
✆ 03-5984 2201

On the main drag, the Continental Café under the veranda of the old limestone Sorrento Hotel is a popular coffee and people-watching stop.

Coppins Tearooms ❷

Sorrento Back Beach car park
✆ 03-5984 5551

On the crashing ocean surf side of Sorrento, Coppins Tearooms, located right within the Mornington Peninsula National Park, gives great views of aspiring surfers and the long wild ocean back beach and reefs, while serving coffee and cakes, lunches, takeaway fish 'n' chips and excellent dinners on summer weekend evenings.

Couta Caffè ❷

26 Ocean Beach Rd, Sorrento
✆ 03-5984 0811

Named after Sorrento's historic fleet of wooden, gaff-rigged barracouta fishing boats, this place has a casual beach-house feel in its airy bar and courtyard, serving plenty of light seafood dishes as well as other meat mains.

The Dunes Restaurant ❿

Surf Beach Rd, Ocean Grove
✆ 03-5256 1944

Spectacularly over-looking the surf beach at Ocean Grove is The Dunes Restaurant, which is hard to beat as a place to enjoy afternoon tea and cakes, or a glass of champagne, *antipasto* and dinner as the sun sets over the crashing surf.

Giuseppe's ⓫

149 Pakington St, Geelong West
✆ 03-5223 2187

This busy little Italian bistro delivers warm ambience, cheap meals and good coffee.

Leonardo's Café ⓬

1373 Murradoc Rd, St Leonards
✆ 03-5257 1844

A smart little restaurant and lunchtime café in the hideaway seaside village of St Leonards where the owners take infinite care with the contemporary food and the atmosphere is drop-in casual during the day and romantic intimacy at night.

The Max Hotel ⓭

2 Gheringhap St, Geelong
✆ 03-5229 5504

It is hard to imagine a more dramatic change than that experienced by The Max Hotel in its transformation from a grand three-storey 1857 gold-rush pub to the smart Max, one of Geelong's hippest nightspots and eateries. Dinner can be classy seafood in the main dining room or a casual barbecue on the balcony.

Ozone Hotel 5

42 Gellibrand St, Queenscliff
✆ 03-5258 1011

Facing the Queenscliff waterfront, the Ozone Hotel is casual and cheap; its **Boat Bar Restaurant**, decorated with historic sepia photos of old steamers and clipper sailing ships, serves elegant modern food.

Port Pier Café 14

6 Piers St, Portarlington
✆ 03-5259 1080

At Portarlington, right down by its jetty complete with fishing boats and offshore mussel farms, is the tasty Port Pier Café serving great Spanish *tapas*, paella and, of course, mussel dishes.

Portsea Pub 4

Portsea Hotel, 3476 Point Nepean Rd, Portsea
✆ 03-5984 2213

This haunt's gently sloping lawns and picnic tables are one of the best places to enjoy a lazy beer or champagne in the sun, while the sprawling hotel serves great seafood on the lawn, out on the veranda or more formally inside.

Queenscliff Terminal Café 5

Queenscliff Car Ferry Wharf
✆ 03-5258 4211

This place may not sound the most romantic location, but is actually a quiet sunny spot tucked away from the bustle of car ferry loading, looking out to The Heads and serving hearty egg-and-bacon breakfasts.

Shells Café 2

85–9 Ocean Beach Rd, Sorrento
✆ 03-5984 5133

A thriving outdoor café and light lunch spot on Sorrento's main street with both indoor and outdoor tables, and surrounded by clothing boutiques, surf shops and a holiday feel.

The Smokehouse 2

182 Ocean Beach Rd, Sorrento
✆ 03-5984 1246

A noisy and happy family restaurant beloved of Portsea and Sorrento's wealthy set for its delicious designer wood-fired pizzas, Caesar salads and bowls of hearty pasta.

Spray Farm Vineyard 14

Spray Farm Rd, Portarlington
✆ 03-5259 1047

Take a drive along the Bellarine Peninsula and drop in for afternoon tea and wine tastings at Spray Farm Vineyard, held under the shady eaves and in the cool garden of the gracious country homestead overlooking Corio Bay.

Vue Grand Hotel 5

46 Hesse St, Queenscliff
✆ 03-5258 1544

The imposing 1881 Vue Grand Hotel boasts a grand ballroom and dining room serving magnificent French-style food – try the daily specials accompanied by Bellarine Peninsula wines.

▲ Shells Café

AROUND PORT PHILLIP BAY
Shops, markets and picnic sites

Shops

Bottoms Up Wine ❷

Shop C, 85–9 Ocean Beach Rd, Sorrento
✆ 03-5984 5962

If looking for local wine to buy cheaply and for quick drinking, drop in here. It stocks cleanskin local wines from the Mornington Peninsula which are bottled in situ in one-litre swing-top lid bottles under enticing labels such as London Bridge Chardonnay or Back Beach dry red.

Just Fine Foods ❷

23 Ocean Beach Rd, Sorrento
✆ 03-5984 4666

The most popular gourmet deli and café in Sorrento is always packed with coffee lovers sitting outside under umbrellas watching the world pass by, and inside with locals desperate to buy its pâtés, pies, gourmet sandwiches, soups and its famous vanilla slice.

Maggie's Kitchen ❺

56 Hesse St, Queenscliff
✆ 03-5258 4141

The cooking smells wafting out of little Maggie's Kitchen are impossible to ignore – this is the place to buy all your favourite home-made tomato chutneys, relishes, pickled onions, strawberry jams and marmalades, as well as old-fashioned sweets such as humbugs, acid drops, boiled fruit drops, extra-strong peppermints and multi-coloured rock sticks.

Mondo ⓯

222 Pakington St, Geelong
✆ 03-5229 7338

The best deli in this area is Mondo, which is well stocked with Spanish meats, Italian olive oils and vinegars, farmhouse cheese from Timboon and Gippsland, and an excellent range of fresh coffee.

Q Food Gourmet Deli ❺

Shop 4, Hobson St, Queenscliff
✆ 03-5258 1101

This is run by a former chocolate and pastry chef, Verity Roberts, and stocks the most delectable fresh tapinades, gourmet breads, homemade pastas, imported and Australian cheeses, fresh *nori* seaweed and Asian noodles and, of course, homemade chocolates and pastries.

Queenscliff Seafoods ❺

4 Wharf St, Queenscliff
✆ 03-5258 1969

To buy fresh fish, crayfish, mussels and scallops on the wharf where the fishing fleet ties up, try Queenscliff Seafoods.

Red Hill Cool Stores ⓰

Station Rd, Red Hill South
✆ 03-5931 0133

This old apple storage shed is now a trendy food barn selling local wines, pâtés, dips, preserves, cakes, take-away casseroles and pasta sauces, as well as local crafts and handmade furniture.

Scicluna's of Sorrento ❷

31 Ocean Beach Rd, Sorrento
✆ 03-5984 4866

This place sells some of the most tender beef and lamb available in Victoria direct from Prom Meats in South Gippsland, as well as a full range of Italian sauces and quality fresh fruit and vegetables.

Sunny Ridge Strawberry Farm ⓱

Corner of Flinders Rd and Shands Rd, Main Ridge
✆ 03-5989 6273

This is the place to visit for picking your own fresh strawberries with a real farm taste, as well as to pig out on strawberry ice cream, strawberry pancakes, and even strawberry sparkling wine and strawberry liqueur.

Ye Olde Worlde Lolly Shoppe ❷

168 Ocean Beach Rd, Sorrento
☎ 03-5984 5455

For the sweet-toothed, this store may have a dreadful name but is a treasure trove of English sweets, boiled lollies, real fudge, long liquorice lengths, genuine gobstoppers, sherbet bombs and incomparable Ernest Hillier chocolates.

Markets

Red Hill Community Market ⓲

Red Hill Recreation Reserve
☎ 03-5988 4424

▲ Sunny Ridge Strawberry Farm

Open: Sept–May first Sat of the month 0800–1300

This fantastic market can take hours to wander around, with its stalls selling fresh fruit and vegetables, homemade preserves, cakes and scones, local wines, honey and pâté, and an extensive range of local arts and crafts.

Picnic sites

Arthurs Seat ❶

The view from the top of Arthurs Seat above Dromana, as well as its extensive Australian native gardens and marked walks, is hard to beat.

Beaches

Picnic on any of the gentle front beaches with their golden sands from **Dromana** to **Portsea** ⓳. Otherwise, any of the calm beaches ringing the bay beaches from **St Leonards** to **Portarlington** ⓴ have swimming and paddling, or tackle the sand dunes and surf at **Point Lonsdale** ㉑, **Ocean Grove** ❿ and **Torquay** ㉒. In Geelong **Eastern Beach** ㉓ is a favourite swimming spot.

Bushrangers Bay ㉔

Between Cape Schanck and Flinders

The walk to secluded Bushrangers Bay through banksia groves is perfectly lovely.

Cape Schanck ㉕

Cape Schanck Rd, behind Boneo

Along the rugged back beach coast, all now protected by the Mornington Peninsula National Park, the lighthouse and cliffs of Cape Schanck are impressive, although often windswept.

Geelong Botanic Gardens ㉖

The extensive and shady Geelong Botanic Gardens on the headland above are beloved of all Geelong walkers, gardeners and picnickers.

Mornington Peninsula tip ㉗

Visit the tip of Mornington Peninsula and view the scary Rip through the national park gates just beyond the Portsea shops.

Red Hill ⓲

At Red Hill many of the wineries encourage picnickers.

Swan Bay ㉘

On the Bellarine Peninsula the shores of Swan Bay behind Queenscliff offer excellent water-bird watching, while there is a steam train for children at the weekends.

Around Port Phillip Bay | 85

Gourmet country retreats

Weekending in style

Victoria is a compact state and Victorians love to spend weekends away at country bed and breakfasts (B&Bs) and gourmet retreats, indolently enjoying fine scenery and open fires, mingled with great food and good wines.

In the goldfields hill country of central Victoria is the highly acclaimed **Lake House** at Lake Daylesford (*King St, Daylesford; ✆ 03-5348 3329; ◉ drive west on the Western Hwy towards Ballarat, turn right to Daylesford at Ballan; open: daily, lunch 1200–1500, dinner 1900–late; reservations essential; all credit cards accepted; Modern Australian;* ❸❸❸). The dining room is a true room with a view, while drinks at sunset with the kookaburra chorus are another treat.

North of Ballarat, in the wine-growing region of the Pyrenees near Avoca, **Warrenmang Vineyard Resort** (*Mountain Creek Rd, Moonambel; ✆ 03-5467 2233; ◉ drive west on the Western Freeway to Ballarat, head north on the Sunraysia Hwy through Avoca to Moonambel; open: daily, lunch 1200–1430, dinner 1900–2130; reservations essential; VISA ⬛ American Express; Modern Australian;* ❸❸❸) has a central rustic brick and timber restaurant that overlooks the vineyards. The Pyrenees hare is the house speciality and vegetarians are well catered for.

Perched on a ridge overlooking Lake Eildon is the internationally acclaimed **Eucalypt Ridge** (*Skyline Rd, Eildon; ✆ 03-5774 2033; ◉ drive east on the Maroondah Hwy, through Healesville to Alexandra; open: weekends and midweek by prior arrangement only, all inclusive accommodation and dining; reservations essential; VISA ⬛ American Express; Modern Australian;* ❸❸❸), offering the ultimate in a luxury weekend, with guests enjoying the finest food and wine that money can buy.

Past Mansfield by the Howqua River is the country getaway beloved by Melbourne's real foodies – **Howqua Dale Gourmet Retreat** (*Howqua River Rd, via Mansfield; ✆ 03-5777 3503; ◉ take either the Melba or*

▲ The Lake House on Lake Daylesford

Maroondah Hwy to Mansfield, then continue towards Merrijig; open: by prior arrangement only, all inclusive weekend rates; reservations essential; all credit cards accepted; Modern Australian regional; ❸❸❸). This hideaway is a magnificent place to enjoy good food and wine in the Australian Alps, or you can book for one of the special cookery weekends.

Further north in the heart of the Rutherglen wine-growing region is **The House at Mt Prior** (*Howlong Rd, Rutherglen; ✆ 02-6026 5256;* 🅿 *drive up the Hume Hwy through Wangaratta and turn off at Sprinhurst for Rutherglen, or catch the country train from Spencer St Station in Melbourne for Wangaratta and take a bus; open: daily, lunch from 1230, dinner from 1900; reservations recommended;* 💳 💳; *Modern Australian;* ❸❸), a towering mansion on the hill overlooking Rutherglen. Its hostess Tricia Hennessy is one of the northeast's best chefs, cooking regional fare such as lamb shanks, duck and trout.

For gourmet travellers keen to explore the spectacular Great Ocean Road, **Chris' Beacon Point Restaurant** (*Skenes Creek Rd, Apollo Bay; ✆ 03-5237 6411;* 🅿 *take the Great Ocean Rd from Geelong and Torquay to Apollo Bay; open: daily, lunch 1200–1430, dinner 1800–2100; reservations essential; all credit cards accepted; Modern Australian;* ❸❸) is the ideal place to stop and stay the night. Perched above Apollo Bay, it offers both lunch and dinner daily. Chris' owner, Chris Talihmanidis, is a food legend and, not surprisingly, seafood fresh from the local fishing fleet is the restaurant's speciality.

On the opposite side of the State in East Gippsland is **Powerscourt Country House** (*Maffra-Stratford Rd, Maffra; ✆ 03-5147 1897;* 🅿 *drive east on Monash Freeway and then Princes Hwy through Warragu and Traralgon, and turn right after Rosedale for Maffra; open: dinner daily from 1800, lunch Sun only from 1200; reservations recommended; all credit cards accepted; Regional;* ❸❸), an elegant 1855 Victorian homestead. Its fixed-price dinner starts with aperitifs in the lounge, followed by four courses in the ballroom dining room.

Mildura on the lazy Murray River may be a long way from Melbourne, but it is a trip that is well worth the effort. One reason to go there is to stay at the venerable Grand Hotel, and enjoy the hospitality of **Stefano's** (*Seventh St, Mildura; ✆ 03-5023 0511;* 🅿 *more than five hours drive from Melbourne via the Sunraysia Hwy, or fly from Tullamarine daily; open: dinner Mon–Sat from 1900; reservations recommended; all credit cards accepted; Northern Italian;* ❸❸), where Italian chef and food celebrity Stefano di Pieri cooks up local Sunraysia produce using ancient family and regional Italian recipes.

> This hideaway is a magnificent place to enjoy good food and wine in the Australian Alps.

Food etiquette and culture

MANNERS
Australia is both a relaxed yet sophisticated place in which to live and work. Fortunately, its eating and dining culture follows the same rules – or lack of them – and food etiquette is neither strict nor rigid, except in the most formal of restaurants. Basically, no one will really mind if you use the wrong knife to butter your bread, or dribble some sauce when trying to twist the spaghetti on to the fork, as long as your manners are polite and polished and demeanour always courteous to even the most lowly of waiters. **Egalitarianism** and **good manners** count for much more in Australian dining rooms than knowing which way to drape the linen napkin neatly over your lap.

OPENING TIMES
Most Melbourne restaurants serve meals until 2200 and many until much later. In general, most people when dining out in restaurants would start ordering their drinks and eating their meals between 1930 and 2100, unless grabbing an early bite before going out to a show. However, traditional pubs tend to serve their meals only from 1800 until 2000.

Because Melbourne has so many theatres and arts venues, some restaurants will offer a choice of two **sittings** for dinner. For travellers on a **budget**, cheaper dinner deals are often offered by some of the most expensive restaurants, with the proviso that they start dining around 1800 and have finished their meal by 2000, when the normal evening dinner rush hour begins.

EATING HABITS
Restaurant lunches are popular with both the business crowd and workers looking to grab a cheap and relaxed *foccacia* or bowl of 'spag bol' as a change from the usual sandwich. **Lunch** in Australia tends to be eaten between 1230 and 1400. After-lunch siestas are not part of the Australian culture; the standard work day for most workers starts at 0900 and ends at 1700. During the morning it is traditional to buy a strong coffee from a nearby café at around 1100. The American habit of eating-out for **breakfast** is also catching on in Melbourne, with many cafés open

▲ Jimmy Watson's

for trade from 0700. More leisurely and later breakfasts are especially popular at weekends, when café tables are full of young people eating eggs and bacon over the Sunday papers, and with many cafés serving filling **brunches** that often extend to midday.

SMOKING

Smoking is not a habit that is either widespread or greatly tolerated in Australia, and litigation is growing against public places that have fostered 'passive smoking' contamination. Although most pubs still allow smoking in their public bars, many restaurants have banned smoking entirely, or have separate **smoking and non-smoking areas**. A few of the more formal restaurants have introduced rules that allow patrons to light up after 2000; however, in general, the trend is for a tightening of restrictions against smoking in eating and public places.

DRINKING

Finding a good glass of wine or beer to drink in Melbourne at any time of the day or night is not difficult. Melbourne is the home of the most **liberal licensing laws** in the country, as well as the birthplace of the wine bar culture, and most restaurants and bars can serve glasses of beer or wine at all times of the day or evening. It is a culture that has made the pleasant and civilised pastime of slowly sipping a drink after work, while the sun goes down, the river sluggishly slides past and the world goes by, very popular amongst Melburnians of all ages.

Melbourne is also the city that, in the restrictive 1950s, broke the mould by introducing Australia's first – and quirky – **BYO laws**. For many years the dominant and preferred licensing system for most Melbourne restaurants, BYO (it stands for 'Bring Your Own') rules meant that diners could bring along their favourite wines, either homemade or bought down the road at the local pub, to the restaurant, rather than having to pay ridiculously high mark-up prices for wine at licensed restaurants. It was a BYO culture designed to encourage good drinking with good eating – and for many years earned Melbourne its reputation as the wine capital of Australia. While most restaurants are fully licensed, if you have a favourite bottle of wine at home or in your hotel room that you would particularly like to drink with your meal, it is worth asking the restaurant you have chosen if they accept BYO wine, as most still do, even if they don't advertise the fact any longer.

Menu decoder

The vast majority of restaurateurs appear to have little interest in alienating patrons with intimidating gastronomy-speak. Whatever the cuisine, it's rare to find a menu in which the foreign name for a dish isn't accompanied by a plain English explanation. That said, this user-friendliness hasn't robbed most cuisines of their authenticity, with 'Westernised' flavours decidedly frowned upon.

MODERN AUSTRALIAN

Most Australian restaurants, bistros, bars and up-market hotels, unless clearly offering another cuisine, serve Modern Australian fare. This style has really only emerged since the 1970s, as Australian chefs have embraced their nation's multicultural origins and its proximity to Asia. A typical Modern Australian menu includes dishes that combine ingredients, spices and flavours from a multitude of different cuisines and cultures. The creators of these dishes use the term 'fusion' for this style of cooking; more humble gourmands would see it simply as a blend of the best ideas, flavours and ingredients from around the world.

Wrap your tastebuds around fresh coral trout, cooked in lime, coriander and coconut milk and served with Hokkien noodles; fresh Tasmanian oysters accompanied by a light dressing of *wasabi*, soy and lemongrass; or fillet steak presented on a bed of polenta and served with *bok choi* and *choko*.

Typically, Modern Australian fare makes the most of the local fresh ingredients, a practice that's laying the foundation of increased regionalisation of the cuisine. In Victoria, a rack of Kiewa Valley lamb may be drizzled with a rich *jus* made from local Yarra Valley plums and Shiraz and served with asparagus freshly picked from the market gardens near Melbourne.

'TRADITIONAL' AUSTRALIAN

Traditional Australian food is another matter entirely. Served mainly in classic Australian pubs, this is 'working man's tucker'. Whether served for lunch ('counter lunch') or dinner ('counter tea'), the fare is unadorned, uncomplicated, not always healthy but excellent value. Expect large servings of rump steak and chips, roast lamb and three veg, steak sandwiches, fish and chips, pies and, possibly, a house pasta. It's practically mandatory to wash down the meal with a cold beer (Australian lager).

COUNTER MEALS AND TAKEAWAYS

barra – fresh barramundi, usually served grilled

▲ Meat pie

'dead horse' – tomato sauce

fishermen's basket – a mix of battered fresh fish, scallops, calamari, prawns and chips

meat pie – pastry pies filled with a runny beef mince and gravy mixture

pie floater – meat pie sitting in a bowl of pea soup

potato scallops/cakes – battered, deep-fried slices of potato often ordered with fish and chips

steak sandwich – rump steak between two slices of white bread

BUSH TUCKER

damper – crusty, unsweetened bread or roll, traditionally fashioned from flour and water and cooked in the ashes of a campfire

lemon myrtle – small bush berry used like a herb, often served with fish

quandong – small purple fruit that makes a jam or a tasty sauce, often served with meats

wattleseed – popular as an ice-cream flavouring

SEAFOOD

Moreton Bay bug – Queensland crustacean halfway between a prawn and a crayfish in size and of similar flavour

pipi – small bivalve mollusc with butterfly-winged shells; flesh tastes a bit like mussel

sashimi – sliced raw fish, on the menu in all Japanese restaurants and many others serving Modern Australian fare

CHINESE

cha siu bao – glazed, steamed buns filled with sweet barbecued pork

darn tarts – golden brown egg custard tarts

dim sum – small dumplings, steamed or fried, with sweet or savoury fillings

dow foo – deep-fried tofu (bean curd)

fong chau – chicken feet, served barbecued, boiled or braised

Hokkien noodle – round yellow wheat noodles

pai gwut – spare ribs in black bean sauce

Peking duck – crispy-skinned duck wrapped in pancakes with spring onions, cucumber and plum sauce

tsun guen – spring rolls, meat or vegetarian fillings

ITALIAN
antipasti – hors-d'oeuvres
biscotti – sweet biscuits, perfect with an after-dinner espresso
focaccia – flat bread
fritatta – omelette containing vegetables, cheese and seasonings
gnocchi – pasta-like dumplings, usually made with potato flour
insalata – salad
pesto – basil, garlic, pinenuts, parmesan cheese and olive oil paste
pollo – chicken
prosciutto – dry-cured ham
risotto – rice dish
scallopine – thin slices of veal

VIETNAMESE
bun – more complex, full meal soup with noodles, meat, vegetables, lemongrass and other flavours, traditionally from Hue in central Vietnam
ca – fish
cuon – rice
muc – squid
pho – simple clear soup (pronounced 'fer') that contains noodles and other ingredients; varieties include *pho ga* (chicken) and *pho bo* (beef)
vit – duck

Recipes

The following two recipes are both seafood recipes. The first is a delightful recipe for fried oysters from **Hagger's** restaurant in South Yarra; the second uses barramundi (the Aboriginal word for 'fish with large scales'), a favourite and sizeable fish from the tropical river estuaries of northern Australia. It is also known as giant perch in African, Asian and South American waters. The barramundi *cartoccio* baked in a paper parcel is a chef's special at Toorak Road's **Café e Cucina** restaurant.

Hagger's fried oysters

Serves 6 as a starter

INGREDIENTS

36 freshly shucked or half-opened oysters, with their shells

For the cucumber pickle:
1 large Lebanese cucumber, cut into 2mm thick slices
1 large white onion, thinly sliced
¼ cup of salt
220g (1 cup) caster sugar
100 ml white-wine vinegar
1 tbsp toasted brown mustard seeds
½ tsp turmeric powder

For the wasabi cream:
1 tbsp *wasabi* paste
1 tsp white-wine vinegar
1 tsp caster sugar
2 tsp pouring cream

For the beer batter:
375 ml light beer
1 egg, lightly beaten
2½ tbsp olive oil
1 tsp sea salt
¼ tsp ground white pepper
300g (2 cups) self-raising flour

For deep-frying:
150g (1 cup) cornflour
peanut oil or safflower oil (deep-fry)

For serving:
salad leaves or rock salt
pickled ginger

First make the **cucumber pickle** by combining the sliced cucumber, onion and salt in a bowl. Line a sieve with muslin, fill with this cucumber mixture, and refrigerate for an hour. Rinse cucumber mixture, then pat dry with absorbent paper. Put cucumber mixture in a stainless steel saucepan. Add remaining pickle ingredients and stir over low heat until the sugar dissolves. Spoon into sterilised jars and seal while hot. Cool to room temperature and then refrigerate (this mixture will keep for up to one month). Bring to room temperature before using.

For the *wasabi cream*, combine all the ingredients in a small bowl and mix well.

For the **beer batter**, first combine all the ingredients except the flour, and whisk to combine. Gradually whisk in the flour to form a batter of pouring-cream consistency, then refrigerate until needed.

Take the **fresh oysters**, and carefully remove the oyster flesh from the shell. Pat both the oysters and their shells dry with absorbent paper.

Arrange the salad leaves or rock salt on six serving plates, and lay six empty oyster shells on each plate. Fill each oyster shell with cucumber pickle.

Heat the peanut or safflower oil in a large saucepan or wok to 180°C. Toss the oysters in cornflour, shake off excess, then dip in the beer batter mix. Deep-fry the battered oysters in batches for 2 to 4 minutes, or until crisp and golden, and then drain on absorbent paper.

Put the oysters back in their shells, on top of

94 | Recipes

the cucumber pickle, and place a small dab of **wasabi** cream on top of each. Serve immediately with pickled ginger, while oysters are still warm.

Barramundi *cartoccio*

Serves 4

This main course is described in Italian as barramundi stuffed with lemon, olive and rosemary, and baked in a paper parcel. While the chef at Café e Cucina uses baking paper or parchment paper, Aborigines traditionally used to wrap the whole barramundi fish in the papery bark of the giant river melaleuca trees.

INGREDIENTS

4 baby barramundi fish (about 350g to 400g each), scaled, gutted and washed

40 x 60cm sheets of parchment or baking paper

4 rosemary sprigs, about 15cm long each

40ml extra virgin olive oil

sea salt

steamed vegetables to serve

For the stuffing:

240g Italian-style white bread

50g kalamata pitted olives

2 tsp of grated lemon rind

1½ tbsp extra virgin olive oil

Make the **stuffing** by first removing the crusts from the bread, cutting it into small pieces and processing in a blender until it is fine crumbs. Transfer the breadcrumbs to a bowl, and process the olives until puréed. Using your fingertips, rub the olive purée and lemon rind into the breadcrumbs, while slowly adding the olive oil until it is all well combined. Season stuffing further to taste. Divide the barramundi stuffing among the four fish, filling the cleaned inner cavity.

Place a single **barramundi** in the middle of a sheet of paper, with its head at your left and the opening facing away from you. Top with a sprig of rosemary. Bring the two long edges of the paper together to join above the fish, and then fold the baking paper in 1cm-wide sections towards the filled side until the paper is about 2cm above the fish. Twist the short ends of the paper tightly like a bon-bon (cracker).

Put all four of the paper-wrapped barramundi on a large oven tray and bake at 250°C for 15 to 20 minutes, or until the paper is puffed and the fish is tender.

Arrange the paper parcels on four plates. Using scissors, cut the paper open, drizzle the fish with extra virgin olive oil, sprinkle with sea salt and serve with the steamed vegetables.

Recipes | 95

Published by Thomas Cook Publishing
Thomas Cook Holdings Ltd
PO Box 227
Thorpe Wood
Peterborough PE3 6PU
United Kingdom

Telephone: 01733 503571
Email: books@thomascook.com

Text © 2001 Thomas Cook Publishing
Maps © 2001 Thomas Cook Publishing

ISBN 1 841570 90 7

Distributed in the United States of America by the Globe Pequot Press, PO Box 480, Guilford, Connecticut 06437, USA

Publisher: Donald Greig
Commissioning Editor: Deborah Parker
Map Editor: Bernard Horton

Project management: Dial House Publishing
Series Editor: Christopher Catling
Copy Editor: Lucy Thomson
Proofreader: Jan Wiltshire

Series and cover design: WhiteLight
Cover artwork: WhiteLight and Kaarin Wall
Text layout: SJM Design Consultancy, Dial House Publishing
Maps prepared by Polly Senior Cartography

Repro and image setting: PDQ Digital Media Solutions Ltd
Printed and bound in Italy by Eurográfica SpA

Written and researched by: **Sue Neales**

The author would like to thank Tourism Victoria, Queen Victoria Market, Crown Casino and all the restaurant and café owners.

The photographers would like to thank the following places: Arirang Mongolian Barbecue, Dicken's Bar, The Grand Hyatt Hotel, Joe Bananas, Kublai's Mongolian Fresh Grilled, Lai Ching Heen Restaurant, Man Wah, The Peak Café, Peking Garden, The Peninsula and Super Star Seafood Restaurant.

We would like to thank Sue Neales, Bruce Postle and those organisations who kindly supplied the photographs used in this book. In addition, thanks to Lake House, Daylesford (page 86), Valerie Martin (page 95) and Tourism Victoria (pages 24, 33, 61, 63, 73, 77 and 81). The copyright of each photograph resides with the photographer.

All rights reserved. No part of this publication may be reproduced, stored in a retrieval system or transmitted, in any form or by any means, without the prior permission of the publishers.

The contents of this book are believed to be correct at the time of printing. Establishments may open, close or change and Thomas Cook Holdings Ltd cannot accept responsibility for errors or omissions, or for the consequences of any reliance on the information provided. Descriptions and assessments are given in good faith but are based on the author's views and experience at the time of writing and therefore contain an element of subjective opinion which may not accord with the reader's subsequent experiences. The opinions in this book do not necessarily represent those of Thomas Cook Holdings Ltd.